MW01492084

May God always hold you in the palms of His hands and may His Angels be forever at your side to guide you across the broken bridges of life.

God Bless you

Sincerely

Jay LaPlant

ANGEL GABRIEL
A TRUE STORY

WRITTEN AND EXPERIENCED
BY Joy LaPlante

Copyright © 1999 by Joy LaPlante

All rights reserved. No part of this book may be used; reproduced, or transmitted in any manner whatsoever without permission in writing from the publisher or author except in the case of brief quotations embodied in critical articles and reviews.

To order more books contact
La-Plant Publishing, P.O. Box 112. Petersburg Michigan 49270
Or Email at angels@cass.net

First Printing: February 1999
Second Edition: November 1999

10 9 8 7 6 5 4 3 2

ISBN# 0-9670356-0-0

*This book is in memory of the 29 people who died on Flight 3272. January 9,1997
And to all of the firemen, police, rescue workers and anyone who was involved and dedicated their time on and off the field that day and for months after.*

Also to my nephew Shane Rogers who lost his fight with cancer in January of 1999.

Notes from the Author

My name is Joy LaPlante and I would like to tell you a little about myself. I was raised in a little town in Michigan.

My parents are Richard and Joyce Rogers. I am the youngest of five children. I have two brothers and two sisters, four nieces and six nephews.

I have three wonderful children of my own. I am married to a wonderful man that has six children, fourteen grandchildren and one great grandchild. We live on a farm and raise racehorses.

My mother raised us to believe in God. We did not belong to any one church. Mom always told us kids that we could get baptized when we were old enough to choose what religion we wanted to be. In 1992, I chose to be Catholic and was Baptized.

I was taught when I was younger that there were angels. My grandmother had a picture of a lady angel that was watching over two little children walking across a broken bridge. I loved this picture. But I had always thought that angels were for special people and I didn't feel that I was special enough for God to give me one of my own.

Or maybe, I felt that I wasn't going to walk across any broken bridges and didn't really need one. But I now know, that life is a broken bridge, and God has given everyone of us an angel of our own. To watch over us so we will not fall through the broken bridges of life.

I don't know why, God and Gabriel choose me to do this wonderful thing for them. But, I feel honored that they did. People ask me how do I know what path to choose when things come up in my life. My answer is the one that is in front of me. Remember that even if things look impossible, they are not. God will always put people in our path to take us to the next passage of our destiny. All we have to do is pray, listen, and follow Gods answer. We all have our own free will, to chose right from wrong left from right. And may you always find the right road.

May God bless you

My thanks to so many Earthly Guardian Angels

I would like to start with thanking my wonderful husband and my beautiful children for not putting me away in a hospital somewhere and for finally believing in me.

Also my Mom and Dad, for being such great Parents. My sisters, and brothers. Without all of you, I would not be the person that I am today.

Also, Thank you to my husband's family.

Thank you, Lynn, Sandy, Adam, Nathan, John, Thad. And Deadalus Art Foundry.
Lynn without you none of this would have been possible. Thank you for being such a wonderful soul. God bless all of you.

And to: Norm and Ginny Willcox, Dick Bryant, and Ed Polling. I know that God sent all of you to watch over me during a very difficult time in my life. I will never forget what you did for me and my children. I thank you from the bottom of my heart. You were all truly my angels when I needed you most.

I would also like to give thanks to:

All the Firemen and women, Police, Rescue workers, etc...all who serve God's people out of the goodness of your hearts.

All the WW1, WW2, Vietnam vets and all those who are in the service and sacrifice yourselves for our freedom. God Bless All of you.

And to my dear friends, Linda Daily and Paula Hunter, thank you both for not being afraid to follow God when he sent you both to me, and for helping me edit this book.

Linda, I thank you and Bill for the idea for the prayer cards and prayer.

Paula, I thank you for helping me spread the prayer cards throughout the world.

My list of people to thank could go on and on, so I will end it here.
If you are an Earthly Guardian Angel, I also thank you.

God our Father in a wonderful way You
guide the work of angels and men.
May those who serve You constantly in heaven
keep our lives safe from all harm here on earth.
Grant this through our Lord Jesus Christ, your
Son who lives and reigns with You and the Holy
Spirit, one God, for ever and ever Amen.

[29th, Romans Missal]

THE PLANE CRASH
January 9, 1997

It was the beginning of the New Year. Outside it was cold, windy and snowing. Inside, I was counting my blessings for a warm house and thinking how glad I was that I didn't have to go outside. I was startled by the sound of my phone ringing. It was my good friend, Honey.

"Joy, did you hear what happened?"
"No, what?" I answered.
"I turned on my police scanner," she continued, her voice serious.
"Joy, there has been a plane crash!"
I felt my heart fall into my stomach as Honey continued. "They're saying it's in a field in Ida." (Ida is a small town six or seven miles down the road from us).

We listened to what was being said on the scanner and could hear a fireman's voice quivering as he spoke.

"We don't know what kind of plane this is, but it looks like a disaster."

My heart sank as low as it could go. I fought back the tears. "I hoped there are survivors. You know when you hear about crashes and you always say 'God that must be terrible', but when it happens this close to you, it hits you a lot harder.

The fireman spoke again, **"Call in Petersburg, Deerfield and Monroe. Put everybody else on standby, we're going to need help. We need to find out what type of plane this was and how many were on it."**

"Honey, maybe it's not a big plane. Maybe it's one of those small ones that only hold two or three people."

"Joy, I don't think they would be calling for that much help for a small plane, do you? Listen to the distress in the firemen's voices. I'm afraid it is a big plane." Then she added, "You know, I'm surprised that this has not happened before now, with us being in the flight pattern of Detroit Metro Airport."

Just then the fireman's urgent voice on the scanner interrupted us.

"We need to go to another channel."

After that, we could no longer hear what was going on and, instinctively, we both knew this was a bad plane crash.

I sat in front of the TV and waited for more news. Honey and I talked more throughout the night, saying to each other how bad we both felt for those rescue workers, who were out there looking for survivors in the middle of the field. The temperature had been steadily dropping and

it was now well below zero. The snow was
still falling and the wind kept blowing.
I prayed urgently that they would find
survivors and also for the families of the
people on board.

Later, we heard that none of the 29
people on board made it. Every night when
I went to bed, I continued to pray for all of
those involved. As I prayed, I could hear
that north wind slamming into the side
of the house trying to come through the
windows. As the windows shook I would
pray harder for the rescue workers who were
still out there at the crash site, knowing how
traumatic it must be for them all.

GABRIEL
Thursday
January 23,1997

It was during the night that I felt the presence of someone standing over me, watching me. I was afraid to open my eyes for fear of what I would see. I just knew if I opened my eyes there would be someone standing there looking at me. I laid there thinking, maybe it was the spirit of my grandmother or grandfather, but somehow I knew it wasn't. I started saying The Lord's Prayer and then I started praying that what ever was there would go away.

However, just then, with my eyes closed. I saw the most beautiful face I had ever seen. His eyes were as blue as the sky on a day full of sunshine with no clouds. The blue part of his eyes had purple running through it and gold flecks that sparkled. At first I just stared at his eyes in total awe.

Then I realized my eyes were open and the feeling of love was overwhelming. So overwhelming in fact, that I thought my chest and heart was going to explode. I was no longer scared. I looked at him and said "Hello".

He smiled and said ***"Hello Joy."***

As he spoke, I could feel myself melt inside. I had such a love for this person that no words can truly explain the depth of it. I felt as if I had known him all my life. I kept staring at him in wonder, looking him over from head to toe. His hair was golden brown, with bright golden highlights, just like those in his eyes. It was like looking into the sun yet it didn't hurt my eyes.

I reached up and touched his hair. It was as soft as a down feather.

I knew in my heart and soul that I had just touched something from heaven. My emotions ran so fast throughout my body.

I couldn't keep up with them.
"Did I die?" I asked.

He smiled and said gently, *"No."*

"Then did God send you?"

"Yes."

I continued to look at him.
"Did I do something wrong?" As I asked this, my stomach started to ache with anticipation, like a kid being called down to the principal's office. Then I looked back into his smiling eyes and knew that he was not here to be my judge. My heart filled with song again. I asked him what his name was.

"Gabriel." he answered.

Oh my, you are so beautiful, I thought in awe, then realized that I had said it out loud. I looked at Gabriel.

"Well if I didn't die, or do something wrong, then why did you come to me?"

"I'm here in answer to your prayers."

"Which one? I pray for so many people everyday."

Then I reminded myself, *don't exaggerate to this messenger from God. I'm sure he knows that I don't pray everyday... but he does know that I try to.*

I looked at him.
"Well I try to pray everyday."

Gabriel looked at me with a warm, understanding smile and held his hand out.

"Take my hand and come with me."

I did as he asked and as we walked, he spoke to me. *"Did you know, that when you pray and your heart is sad, not only do we hear your prayers but we also feel your pain?"*

"No I didn't, but that is very comforting to know." Then I asked, "Gabriel, is that why we feel better after we pray?"

He smiled at me. *"Yes, we help carry your burdens. Now in your prayers you keep saying that you wish you could do something to help people that are sick of the heart."*

"Yes, are you talking about my prayers for the people on that plane?"

"Yes and others, also."

It seemed so incredible that I could be having this experience, so I just stared at him.

"Now, I have a job for you to do and this will help many people."

Before I could even think I said, "Ok what?"

Then I wondered what could I possibly do that could help a lot of people?

Gabriel looked at me and with his loving smile, *"You will see in time."*

I remember thinking to myself, *Oh my! I didn't even speak and he knew what I was thinking.* We looked at each other. *Can you hear me?* I asked silently. He laughed and answered.

"Yes and you know what? We angels have a sense of humor too."

Just then the word 'angel' hit me like a ton of bricks. My emotions started to run rampant again. I said loudly.

"Angel...ANGEL! Oh my! You're an ANGEL?"

He started laughing *"Yes."*

My voice was still loud as I said, "An Angel from God and you're here talking to me and asking *me* for help?"

He continued to smile at my reaction, *"Yes."*
I thought about this for a moment.
"If you're an angel where are your wings?"

"Do you want to see? Will that help you know that I'm an Angel of God?"

Just then, big beautiful white wings unfolded from his back. I fell to my knees and stared. Then I started to cry.

"You really are an angel sent from God."

Tears of joy rolled down my face as my heart sang praise to God. My mind was full of questions. *What in the world did I ever do in my life to be honored so greatly by God? Why would God send an Angel to me to help him? I'm sure there is someone out there in this world that is far worthier than I for this job, what ever it is.*

I kept staring at Gabriel thinking, *an Angel this is really an Angel before me. Oh my!*

After I gathered up my emotions, I asked quietly, "Gabriel are you real or am I just dreaming, because if I am, I hope I don't wake up. I have never felt this much love and have never seen anything as beautiful as you in my whole life."
Gabriel smiled down at me. *"Yes you have, you just don't remember. And yes, my dear Joy, I am real."*

Then he reached out his hand to me, so I put mine in his. I was standing again.

"Now, we have a lot to do. Are you ready?"

"Yes" I said with eagerness, still amazed at what I was seeing. All that kept going through my mind was *Wow, an Angel!*
As we walked, Gabriel spoke again. *"Now I'm going to show you something and I don't want you to be afraid."*

He led me to what seemed like the edge of a cloud and waved his arm, as if to move the cloud. Then he pointed.

"Look"

At first I wasn't sure what I was looking at. Then I saw lights, lots of them in an open field, and a big tree.
Looking from a distance, I saw people everywhere. I saw the scattered remains of a plane and my heart sank into the pit of my stomach. I realized at that moment what Gabriel was showing me.
I looked at him, "Why are you showing me this?"

Gabriel looked at me with such kindness on his face. *"You could not do what it is that I need of you if you do not understand. Your heart is filled with sadness for those people and I want you to understand that the people who died on that plane did not die. You're so focused on what they went through that you won't be able to do what I need you to if you don't change your sad heart."*

I understood what he was saying so I looked back to where all the commotion was. I could see the eyes of the rescue workers and the reality that was changing their lives. I also felt the hope in their hearts that they would find survivors. This was almost more than I could bear.

Around the rescue workers I saw other people. Their bodies were glowing and they were almost translucent. These people, (with glowing bodies) were also looking around in total disbelief at the scene before them. They were trying to talk to the rescue workers but the workers did not seem to notice them. The people, with glowing bodies, could not understand what was going on. One man with a glowing body was following a fireman around. He kept saying over and over again, "We are fine, we are fine. Why don't you listen to me? Why aren't you looking at me?" His voice was getting distressed but the fireman didn't even acknowledge him.

Then I noticed a woman with a glowing body. She was looking for something near the big tree. Then she smiled. She reached out her arms and picked up a little baby that was sitting on the ground. The baby smiled and raised up his arms for her to pick him up. I could tell this woman was relieved that the baby wasn't hurt.

Then I noticed a man with some kind of uniform on. He had a glowing body too. He was running around to all the other people with glowing bodies. He was checking everyone to make sure they were all right, and was relieved when he found out that everyone was okay. Then he walked up to a fireman and tried to talk to him, but panicked when the fireman didn't reply.

The lady with the baby walked up to this man and said, "I think we died, that is why they cannot hear us."

"No…" he gasped, with total disbelief. "I have too much left to do in my life, I couldn't have died. What about my family? What about…?" He stood there for a moment in resignation, then said, "I guess it really doesn't matter now does it?" The woman gave him an understanding smile.

"Now what? What do we do now?" he asked.

"I don't know, but I'm sure God will lead us home," she replied.

Then I became aware of some things in the distance, flying from the ground to the sky. The only way to explain what this looked like is to imagine birds, thousands of them migrating south for the winter.

Gabriel pointed to this. *"Those are prayers of hope. Prayers for the people on this plane and prayers for the rescue workers."*

That was when I realized that the people with glowing bodies were the people that had died in the plane crash.

Then I heard singing from the distance. Beautiful singing, lovelier than I had ever heard before. Then I saw the Angels lots of them...maybe hundreds or so, coming from heaven. I watched as they went down to the rescue workers. Each angel stood by a person.

"Are those Angels here to help the rescuers?" I asked Gabriel.

"Yes, everybody has their own Angels to help them through everything in their lives. Even the non-believers have their own Angels."

Before I could ask he answered.

"And yes there are some of those down there."

I watched what was happening for a while, then I said, "Gabriel…" He looked at me and before I could say another word he said.

"Just wait and see."

Just like before, he knew my question before I could ask it. Then, there was more singing. But this singing was a little different. It was sweeter. I looked to where the singing was coming from and saw more Angels. These Angels looked a little different. They were brilliant white like the others yet they had color in their gowns, (Like a queen's crown.)

I noticed the people with the glowing bodies had stopped trying to get the attention of the rescue workers. Now their eyes were focused on these Angels. They all started to sing the song that the Angels were singing. I have no idea what this song was, but I do know it was beautiful.

I heard one man say to another, "I told you we didn't make it."

Then the woman with the baby said to them, **"Oh yes! Oh yes we did!"** She smiled and sung as loud as she could as she watched the Angels coming for her and her baby. Then the man looked up, as though in disbelief. But when he saw the Angels coming, his expression turned into one of complete joy. Then he also started to sing as loud as he could.

Maybe this man didn't believe there was a Heaven before, but he does now! I thought to myself.

The Angels had big smiles on their faces as they approached the people, who were standing as still as statues, but they were singing. I could tell they were not afraid of anything anymore. Every single person who had been on that plane had a look on his or her face of ecstatic wonder. They were in total awe. I watched as each Angel went one by one to the person that belonged to them and put out their hands. The people reacted by putting their hands out as well, reaching for their Angel just as a child would for its parent.

The Angels wrapped their wings around the people and took them off to heaven, every single person that was on the plane. This was a sight I will never forget as long as I live.

Then my focus turned to the rescue workers. I could feel the pain that was in their hearts. It was more than I could bear. I looked at Gabriel. "If only they could have seen the Angels take those people to heaven, they would not be feeling so much pain. "Why did you show me this?"

"I showed you this because you cannot do what it is I need you to do, if you have a sad heart. You must see so you <u>do</u> believe that those people went to heaven, so you can lift other's hearts, so they, too, will rejoice to God instead of blaming him."

Gabriel continued, *"There are always people who turn away from God when things like this happen and you are going to help me to help them."*

I looked at Gabriel and said, "But I do believe in God."

Once again, he smiled at me with great understanding. *"I know you do, but trust me, there is a reason I am showing you these things and when the time comes you will know why."*

I wasn't sure at the time why he showed me these things, so I didn't talk about this to anyone, fearing they would say; *yep, now she's really lost her mind!* But as I'm writing this down and reliving it in my mind, I'm beginning to understand.

THE NEXT MORNING

The next morning I woke up and went downstairs to find my husband.

"You're not going to believe this," I said, "but an Angel came to me last night! It was as real as I am standing here talking to you. I remember every little detail."

Bud gave me a look that showed he thought I was crazy and said. "Oh yeah? And what did this Angel want?"

Cautiously, I answered. "Well, he asked me to do something for him."

"What?"

"I don't know. He forgot to tell me." Then Bud asked. "And what was this Angel's name?"

"Gabriel!" I said with excitement.

My husband then said, "Joy, Gabriel is an Archangel and I don't think he's going to come to you."

"Well, maybe it's a different Gabriel. You know I'm sure there is more than one…don't you think?" For a moment, I began to feel unsure of myself because of his disbelief.

Bud walked over to me and patted me on the back and said, "Ok hon." Then he looked at our youngest son and said, "Tyler, get me the phone. I have to call the men in the white coats to come and get your mom."

We both started laughing. Then I said, "I'm telling you the truth but it's ok. You don't have to believe me."

Once again, after seeing Buds reaction, I questioned what I had seen and even panicked a little. I kept thinking, "Gabriel, did you forget to tell me what it was you wanted of me? Or worse, did I forget?" I was sure I had remembered every detail about all he had shown me. But why couldn't I remember what it was he wanted me to do for him? After going over all the details in my mind, I started to think that maybe it really was just a dream. A life-like dream…an awesome dream. After all, why would an Angel come to _me_?"

How could I help as many people as Gabriel had said I would? After all, I'm just a wife, a mother and stable hand. More and more, I started to think Bud was right. It must have been a dream. But I just couldn't get everything that Gabriel showed me out of my mind. Later that day my husband came in from the barn. He looked at me with a smile on his face.

"So what did Gabriel say to you?"

I knew he was trying to pick on me, but I wasn't going to let him. So I just smiled back. "I'm not really sure?" I said.

Friday night;
GABRIEL CAME TO ME AGAIN

Lying in bed that night, trying to go to sleep, I recalled everything I was shown the night before. I was replaying it all in my mind as if it was on TV. To my amazement I was once again experiencing all of the emotions that the rescue workers had felt.

I was aware of their feelings of sadness and being sick to the stomach and once again it was almost more than I could bear. My heart went out to them. I prayed.

If there is something I can do to help these people ease their pain, I will. I don't care if other people think I'm nuts.

Then I remembered seeing the Angels come for the people on the plane. My heart was full of happiness again.

I remember the man who was confused about his beliefs, and then I wondered how many people have felt that same confusion? I wondered how many people die and wished that they had lived better lives and done more good things for others, instead of thinking only of themselves? I'm not saying, for one moment, that the man on the plane was selfish or bad. I think he felt like a lot of people do and was just unsure of an after life. But I know in the end he did believe. This made me feel much better to know that there is always hope for everyone, even at the very end of his or her life. It was good to know God really does love us no matter what. If only people could love each other with unconditional love like that.

When I finally drifted off to sleep, Gabriel came to me again. I awoke and I felt peace and love all around me.

I looked at him and said, "Gabriel, was what you showed me last night real?"

"Yes."

"I am so glad you came back, I was afraid that you had told me what it was you needed me to do and I had forgotten what it was."

Gabriel smiled, *"I didn't tell you last night, because I didn't want to overload you with too much information all at once."*

I was so relieved to hear this. I smiled at him and said, "Well you know, all day I kept thinking that I had lost my mind. I tried to tell my husband and he thought I was nuts. But I only told him about you, I didn't tell him what you showed me. I figured if he couldn't handle the thought of you, I know he couldn't handle what you showed me."

Gabriel just smiled.

"Gabriel, Bud asked me why would an Angel named Gabriel come to you and ask you to help him?"

"And what did you say?"

" I just looked at him and said good question!" Gabriel laughed.
"You and he will see. All of your questions will be answered in time. People, he continued *are going to think what they want to. You can not stop this. But the people who believe in God and in Angels will believe you, so do not be afraid to tell of this experience when you feel comfortable and the time is right for you. Now, there is much work to do."*

"Ok, I'm ready." I said with eagerness.

"Joy I want you to look at my gown.
Do you see how it flows?
Do you see how it gathers in places?"

I nodded.

"I want you to touch my gown where it
gathers. Get the feel of it in your hands."

I did as he asked, I had never felt material like this in my whole life. It was softer than satin.

"Touch my feet, get the feel of them in
your hands."

When I did this I could feel energy, like electricity, run though my hands.

"Touch my hair. Get the flow imprinted on your hands."

I must say I have never felt hair so soft. It was as if it were melting through my fingers it was so soft. I really can't describe this feeling, but as I'm writing about this I can still feel all these things on my hands.

"Put your hands on my face."

I cupped my hands and touched his face. The warmth and love that poured from him made me dizzy. I kept thinking how beautiful he was.

"Touch my wings,"

I have never touched feathers like this before. There are no feathers on this earth to compare them to. Gabriel then took my hands into his.

"Joy, I want you to look at my hands."

I did as he asked. I turned his hands over and looked at them. I ran my hands along his wrists, over his palms, and down each finger. I have never held such beautiful hands. The energy that was coming from them into mine was incredible. I felt as if my whole body and soul was electrified.

"Now close your eyes."

I did as instructed.

"Do you still see everything I have shown you?"

"Yes" I answered eagerly.

"Do you see all the detail?"

"Yes"

"Open your eyes. Now I will tell you why I came to you."

I stared at Gabriel intensely and waited.

"You said to God in your prayers that you wished there was something more that you could do to help people, especially the ones involved with the plane crash."

"Yes, I still wish I could do more to help than just pray. Not that there is anything wrong with praying, but I just wish I could do more."

"I know what you mean and that is exactly what you are going to do."

I smiled at him and thought, *Wow ask and you shall receive.* Then I though, *'Oh my!*

What is it I can do to help people?'
Gabriel laughed at my thoughts. I forgot he could hear them.

"Joy, you can do anything you put your mind to, anybody can."

I laughed now. "Gabriel, have you been talking to my mom?" That is what she always tells me." I was getting more and more anxious to find out what he was going to have me do. "Ok, so what is it I'm going to be doing?"

"It is very simple. You are going to make a statue of me."

As he smiled at me he must have seen the panic in my eyes.

"Don't worry it is all taken care of."

I could feel my heart sinking as fast as the tears were coming into my eyes.

"I'm sorry Gabriel but I don't know how I am supposed to do this" My voice filled with panic. "How will I remember all the things you showed me?" Then Gabriel put his hand on my shoulder.

"Joy, I want you to close your eyes."

I did as he said.

"Do you still see me?"

"Yes", I answered. "But I know that I will forget…" Gabriel stopped me in mid sentence.
"You do not have to worry. Your hands will remember everything you have touched. When you close your eyes you will see everything you have touched and

you will see every detail. Also I will be right by your side to help you."

Gabriel smiled once again. *"You must have faith. Don't worry."*

I thought about this for what seemed like forever. "After I make a statue of you what am I supposed to do with it?"

"You are going to give the statue of me to your firemen. Then you will go from there. I will guide you."

"Ok, but why the firemen?" I asked.

"Remember when I took you to the crash site and I had you experience all of the emotions that they were feeling?"

I nodded.

"A lot of those people wonder why they were put in such a predicament. They wonder why they had to see what they did. Some of them are asking why they keep putting themselves through the heartaches. Some of them are even losing their faith in God, because of the things they have experienced in that field and on a day to day basis. They wonder why they put their mental health on the line and why they make their families suffer along with them. There are a lot of these people all over the world that will only think of the safety and well being of others. These are very special people."

I understood what he was saying to me, but the question kept going through my thoughts, *How is a statue going to help people?*

"Joy I am a healer and a messenger sent by God. You will put me in the path of those who need me so I can help them get back to God. You see when they look at me; I will touch a very special place in their hearts. I will heal them and help them."

"Gabriel, will you only help firemen?"

"No, I will touch everyone's heart who sees me or touches me as well as those who call out to me for help."

This was the last thing I remember Gabriel saying to me.

SATURDAY MORNING

I opened my eyes and lay in bed thinking about this task that I had been told to do. I wondered again if it truly happened. *It sure seemed real.* I laid there gazing at my hands. I could feel everything that I had touched on Gabriel, his face, his gown and his hands. I closed my eyes to see if I could see him just like he said I would be able to. *Yes! I could see him just as plain as day!* Then I thought *'well if I'm losing my mind, this is a pretty good way for it to go!*

I got out of bed and went downstairs to where my husband was. "Guess what? Gabriel came to me again last night."

Bud looked at me like 'oh boy she's lost it now.'

"What did he want this time?"

"He told me that I was to make a statue of him," I explained.

Bud said, "Oh yeah?" I kept looking at him, watching for his reaction. He sounded concerned.

"How are you going to do this, Joy?"

Before I answered him, panic ran through my body. I thought to myself, *How? Oh my! How? Gabriel never told me how I was going to do this and I didn't ask.* What was I going to do now? I closed my eyes. *How Gabriel, how? I forgot to ask you how?*

Then I saw Gabriel's smiling face and I became calm. I looked at my husband and said, "I don't know how yet."

Bud persisted. "What are you going to do with a statue?"

"Oh" I said. "I'm going to give him to our firemen."

"Why?" Bud said, trying to sound patient. "Why the firemen?"

Oh boy here we go. I can see it in his face he doesn't believe me for a moment.

"Because" I said, "they need to know they are out Guardian Angels here on earth. No matter who they are and if you like them or not. If you're dying on a street somewhere, they will be there to save your life if they can. They are always putting their lives on the line for people they don't even know."

Bud stood there looking at me for a moment, then he walked out the door and went to the barn to work.

I remember thinking, *boy I would like to be inside his mind right now. I knew he'd be telling himself, 'she has really lost it'.*

This was the day that Bud would go to get hay for our horses. I had to go to my Mom and Dad's to pick up some barbecue sauce that they make. Bud and I went our separate ways without talking anymore about Gabriel.

At my parents house I said, "Mom, I had a weird…no, not weird…an awesome dream for the last two nights."

She smiled and asked, "What? Tell me."

Eagerly, I began to explain. "An Angel came to me, Mom. It wasn't like a dream at all...it was real. I am sure of it. He came two nights in a row.

Smiling she said, "Well what did he want?"

"He told me to make a statue of him and give him to the firemen and rescue workers." I was excited to be able to talk about my experience, but I could tell by the reaction on her face that I didn't dare say anymore. I stood there waiting for a response. At first she just stared at me. I kept thinking, *this is the same look that was on Bud's face.*

Then Mom looked down at the counter and started talking about something else.

I really wanted to share this with someone but nobody wanted to listen. I picked up the barbecue sauce, told Mom that I had to get going and headed for the door.

"You really don't have to run off, you know. You just got here," she said.

I forced a smile and said, "Yes I do. I have to start cooking the meatballs."

Mom's face showed deep concern. She walked over and gave me a hug and a kiss. Then she cupped her hands around my face, "I love you."

"I love you too, Mom. And I'm not crazy. I did see an Angel."

She smiled and said, "I don't doubt it at all."

I thought to myself, *"well if you could look in the mirror right now at the expression on your face, you would see it was saying the opposite of the words you are saying."*

I went out to the car. Mom and Bud's doubts were starting to rub off. I wondered if I could be going crazy. *Was this the way everyone is going to react? Could I handle this?* I didn't know.

As I was driving I said, *"Gabriel, I know you are real."* I looked at my hands again. I could feel the energy in them. I closed my eyes and I could still see his face. I thought to myself again, *well if I'm not nuts now, I will be soon.*

While I was driving I said out loud in a demanding voice, **"Gabriel if you are real give me a sign and give it to me now!"**

Before I could take another breath the radio got loud and the song 'Angels Among Us,' by Alabama, was playing. My emotions ran away with me. I started to cry and I thought, *"oh my God, Gabriel you are really real!"*

I was crying so hard that I almost pulled off the road but I didn't, I kept driving. I took a deep breath and told myself, *this is just a coincidence.*

Then I said out loud, "Gabriel if I'm suppose to make you and give you to the fire department I want another sign."

I was approaching my house and noticed a car in the driveway, so I wiped the tears away and pulled in. It was Carol Pirolli and her husband. They were there to pick up their daughter and mine. I started to cry again because Carol's husband is a volunteer fireman. I had on dark sunglasses I was hoping that she wouldn't be able to tell that I was crying. As I got out of my car Carol said, "Joy, we're going to take the girls shopping."

I was looking at the ground. Then she said, "Hey, you have never met my husband, have you?"

I walked over to their car and Carol introduced me to Ted. When I shook his hand, electricity ran through my hand all the way up to my shoulder. I started to cry again. I said to them, "Well I'd better go and get the girls."

I was hoping they wouldn't think I was being rude by rushing off but I was afraid that the overpowering emotion could have made me break down right there in front of them. I had to get into the house.

As I opened the door the girls were walking out. I managed to give Leah a kiss and told her that I loved her. I shut the door behind me and walked to the kitchen where I fell apart. I cried like I've never cried before. However, these were tears of excitement, joy, and reality.

I kept pacing around the table. I don't know how many times. I was thinking about the signs that I had just been given.

I had asked for a sign that Gabriel was real and the song "Angels are among us" had played on the radio and then I had asked about giving the statue to the firemen and a fireman was in my driveway.

I said out loud, "Gabriel is this for real? Is this really happening? Or is this all just a coincidence?" The doubts started running through my mind again. *Maybe Bud was right. Why would an Angel come to me? Why would he ask me to do this and not someone else? I'm sure Gabriel that you could find someone more qualified than I am. Someone who knows what they're doing.*

Just then the sound of my words rang in my head. *Doing? Oh my, how am I going to do this?* I realized just then that I was pacing around the table. I started laughing out loud *"Gabriel, if someone walked into the house right now and saw me like this, they would call 911 and have me put away. Then Bud and Mom would say, I knew it! She did lose her mind'."*
"OK, OK… *I get the hint. You want me to make you and give you to the firemen. But how?"*

Then the thought hit me, *I don't know how. I carve stone, but only small things that are no larger than three or four inches around. And I know that you want me to make you at least 4 feet tall.*

"Gabriel", I said aloud, "I could never afford a stone that tall. It would cost me hundreds, maybe even thousands of dollars. Besides it would take me at least ten years to accomplish a task that large! I'm really not too sure about this. "I felt like I was going to be sick to my stomach. I thought, I've already failed before I've even started. Then I heard Gabriel's voice, calm and reassuring.

"You can do anything you put your mind to, if you just believe in yourself."

"Gabriel I do believe, I just don't know how I'm going to do this." His reply was simple but so true. ***"Have faith"***

"Yes, Gabriel you are right, and I am sorry. I will put all of this in the hands of you and God. I will let you lead and I will follow."

THE PHONE CALL

An hour or so later everything was still racing though my mind when the phone rang. It was Lynn she is the owner of a bronzed shop called Deadalus Art Foundry. I had met her when I had taken my stone carving class that I was teaching to her shop. I had shown Lynn some of the stones that I had carved and had asked her if it would be possible to pour some of them in bronze.

She said that she would try, but she didn't know if it would work because the stones were so small. I had told her that I would be willing to work for her to pay for the cost of doing this for me. She laughed and said that she might take me up on my offer.

Lynn was calling to tell me that my stones were finished, then she asked if I would like to come and work for her for a couple of days during the week? I agreed to be there the following Monday morning at nine.

After hanging up the phone I thought, *Now why did I tell her yes? I have a lot of work to do around the farm* and for a second I considered calling her back, but I decided it would be a fun change of pace. *Besides I'd only be working a couple of days a week, so it would be no big deal.*

My thoughts kept returning to how I was going to make Gabriel, when all of a sudden I heard that familiar voice ring in my head.

"TELL HER, TELL LYNN ABOUT ME."

Ok but she's going to think that I'm nuts just like my Mom and Bud. I answered.

SUNDAY AT CHRUCH

It was Sunday. I was kneeling in church saying my prayers.

God, I am your instrument. It was you that put me on this earth and your hands that molded me into the person that I am today. If this is your wish and you want me to make a statue of Gabriel, I will. But, I would like a sign from you, so that I know, without any doubt, that it is your will that I should do this.

All of a sudden my hands felt electrified. This startled me. I guess I wasn't expecting a sign that soon. I knelt there and stared at my hands, aware of the feeling of electricity running though them. I could feel the strength of the emotions running through out my body. This was exactly the same overwhelming feeling I had experienced when I had touched Gabriel.

It was time to sit down so the mass could start, but my thoughts were caught up in all I was experiencing so I was unaware of everyone sitting down.

My daughter touched my shoulder.

"Mom, sit back."

When I did, I could feel the tears in my eyes and wanted to cry, but held on to my emotions. I knew God had answered me. The tears were of happiness, honor and maybe also because I was just a little scared that I might let God and Gabriel down.

I kept thinking *God has just touched me and has given me this task, but I don't know how I am going to do it.*

Just then I heard that beautiful voice again. ***"Don't worry, I am with you. I am always with you. All is taken care of. Have faith."***

I couldn't stop the tears this time. I glanced across at my daughter to see if she had heard the voice. She hadn't.

She looked at me and asked why I was crying? I couldn't speak to answer her.
The tears continued to flow I could not stop them. When I went up for communion and stood in front of Father he looked at me with concern in his eyes, he held up the host and said.

"THIS IS THE BODY OF CHRIST!"

I stared at the host that Father was holding up and it glowed like a light.
"AMEN" I heard myself reply. He placed the host in my mouth and I thought I would explode.
I can only describe the feeling as pure love. It was the same feeling that I had experienced when I was with Gabriel…only now it was more intense. I felt very dizzy.
I almost fell to my knees. I'm not sure how I made it over to the person giving out the wine but I did.

(I felt as if I was being carried).

I looked up and it was my Godmother.
She said, "Joy,

"THIS IS THE BLOOD OF CHRIST!"

Once again I felt dizzy, I was afraid to take
the glass out of her hand for fear I would
drop it. But I did and then again I heard
myself saying "AMEN." As soon as the
Blood of Christ touched my lips, my body
felt as if someone had plugged me into a 220
outlet.

The next thing I knew I was back on my
knees praying at my seat. I was still crying.
I wondered how I had gotten there. I looked
around. Nobody seemed to be looking at
me. So I knew that no one had helped me
get back to my seat. At least, no one in the
physical realm.

When we left church no one said anything to me, so I figured that nobody had noticed that something was going on with me. Then, as I got into the car, Leah said, "Mom, why were you crying?"

At first I told her that I didn't know. Then I said, "Well, I do know but you just wouldn't understand and I can't explain it to you right now, ok."

Thankfully she respected my wishes and didn't ask again even thought it was killing her not to know.

Bud looked at me with concern and asked if I was ok.

"Yes, I said but I will tell you something. I have to make Gabriel and give him to the firemen no matter what anyone says!" Bud just looked at me and I knew he understood that it was something I had to do. I knew, for sure, that this was something God wanted of me and His message was loud and clear.

MONDAY MORNING

I got up with Bud to see him off to work. I told him that I was going up to the foundry to work. He said, "How are you going to do this and take care of the kids and the horses along with everything else?"

"Don't worry," I said, I will manage. After all, I'm use to doing 50 things at once. Besides, if it doesn't work out and it starts interfering with everything else, I will just tell Lynn that I can't come anymore. It's as simple as that. This is something I have to do, I continued. I just can't explain it to you right now, ok?

I could tell from his expression that Bud was troubled that I may be taking on too much. "Joy you're running in too many directions. You have to focus on one thing at a time. "I just smiled at him and said, "I know, and I am."

We kissed and he left for work.

As Bud was pulling out of the driveway I called out, "I *am* focusing on doing one thing and that is making Gabriel. I don't know how yet but that is what I'm doing."

I woke up the kids and sent them off to school, straightened up the house, then went out to feed and put the horses out. Finally, my work was done at home. I was excited yet nervous.

As I drove up there I said aloud, Gabriel, I don't know if I'm going to tell Lynn about you yet. She will think that I'm nuts."

Once again, I heard his voice.

"Tell Lynn about me when you get there."

"Easy for you to say. Are you sure?" I asked? Then I answered myself saying,

"Of course you are and you don't have to answer me."

When I arrived, Lynn was sitting at her desk with a big smile on her face. She asked if I was ready to start.

"Yes," I answered, "but I have to tell you something first."

I sat down in a chair and said, "Lynn we don't know one another well, but I have something to tell you and after I get done you're going to think that I'm nuts and you will probably tell me, "Its ok Joy, I really don't kneed you. You can go home now."

She laughed and said, "No I won't. What is it?"

I took a deep breath and told her my story of how an Angel came to me and told me to make him, then give him to the firemen. The whole time I was telling Lynn my story, she just sat there looking at me.

I couldn't read any reaction on her face because there was none. After I had finished telling her, she sat there for a minute.

"Well, Joy, then you must make him. She answered."

"But how, Lynn?" I could feel the panic growing inside of me.

"Have you ever sculpted before?" she asked. I shook my head no.

"Well, I think you can." She said, "and I will give you everything that you need the clay, the armature and the Styrofoam. You make him and you can give him to the firemen."

"Lynn, there is only one problem. I have no money for this."

She smiled and reassured me that I wasn't to worry. We could work something out. My sense of relief was great and I knew Gabriel had sent Lynn to me.

Right then I felt that she was an angel working on earth "Lynn, I said, I have to have him done by July."

Her eyes widened in surprise.
"This July? Seven months from now?"
"Yes," I nodded. "That is what Gabriel said. I need to give him to the firemen on Community day."

"Well if you get him done by them we will make sure he is ready for Community Day."

I was excited. Things were becoming a lot clearer now that I knew how I was going to make Gabriel. I said confidently,
"I will have him done by them."
I had followed Gabriel's instructions and had told Lynn and now everything seemed to be falling into place so perfectly. Then I added, "Just one more thing, Lynn. What is an armature? And what do you use the Styrofoam for?" She laughed and said, "The armature is the skeleton of a figure.

You use this to get the proportions right. The Styrofoam is to build out from the skeleton so you don't have to use a lot of clay."

"Oh, I laughed, I guess I have a lot to learn don't I?"

She smiled and said, "Yes you do, but it's not hard and I believe you can do this."

I looked at Lynn and said, "Thanks for believing in me. You're the first person I told besides a friend of mine that didn't treat me like I was nuts." Lynn just smiled. I knew that Gabriel couldn't have led me to anyone more perfect for helping me in this task.

As the days went by I got to know everyone that worked at the foundry. There was Sandy, Lynn's right hand woman. She is also an earth bound Angel. I found that I could talk to her about anything and she understood and would answer any questions that I had.

Then there was John, Lynn's right hand man. He is a very intelligent man. So much so, that he intimidated me even though it was unintentional. It was my own insecurities that made me feel this way.

One day John came in and said, "So you want to make a statue? Lynn said that you need me to show you how to make a drawing."

I answered, "Yes, I would really appreciate it. I have no idea how to do it."

"It's very simple, this is how you do it." He took a piece of paper and drew on it. "You have to have so many heads for the body, so many heads for the arms and so many heads for the legs. Understand? Very simple."

Not wanting to look dumb, I said, "Sure I do, thank you." Even thought I had no idea what John was talking about.

He said, "No problem. You're welcome." I walked into the other room and tried to fight back the tears and prayed silently. *"Oh my God, please help me understand."* I didn't want to look dumb in anyone's eyes but it seemed like John was talking in another language! It was hardly surprising that I felt out of my league, when I hadn't even finished high school and I was trying to understand the intellectual explanations of these fine college graduates with degrees.

I realized at that moment just what a sheltered life I had lived. I will say Lynn, Sandy and John never tried to make me feel like I was anything but their equal. It was me. I knew that I wasn't. They gave me the best education of a lifetime while I was with them. They taught me how to work with bronze, make molds and work with wax. I really enjoyed it. I also learned to enjoy different kinds of music. I would say to John every day, "Now explain one more time how to draw a layout." He would explain it over and over. But it still wouldn't sink in. One day he brought me in a drawing that he had made and let me borrow it to look at. I took it home with me over a weekend and studied it till my eyes and brain hurt. I still could not understand it.

On Saturday morning I was determined to understand the drawing John had lent me. My two youngest children, Tyler and Autumn, were watching cartoons when Tyler said, "Mom, look on TV! Isn't that what you're trying to do?"

There was a commercial on, where an animator was teaching children how to draw Judy Jetson. He said, "First you have to figure out the size of Judy's head.

Then her body will be so many heads and her arms will be so many heads and her legs will be so many heads, etc…"

Tyler said, "Mom, I think Gabriel is trying to help you by having that on."

I laughed and said; "Do you think so? Well it's not helping me."

He looked at me with such trust and said, "You can do it Mom, I have faith in you."

There it was again, I thought, *Reminding me about 'faith' once more.*

That commercial must have been on 20 times and every time, Tyler would say, "There it is again mom!" After watching it over and over again, I finally sat down and drew it up. It took me about one hour. To my surprise it was almost perfect, except for some little minor lines. I couldn't believe it! It really hadn't been so hard, after all. *Nerve racking maybe, but not hard.*

I realized Tyler was right.

I could do anything if I would just have a little faith in myself and not be afraid to fail. My faith in God and Gabriel was far stronger than my belief in my own capabilities. Now I knew, with Gabriel there to guide me, I would be fine.

Back at the foundry, Lynn, John and Sandy were working on a statue for the village of Perrysburg, in Ohio. The statue was of Commodore Perry. They had to sculpt him out of clay before they could start making a mold. The clay I needed to make Gabriel was being used on the Commodore, so I had to wait until they were done.

Meanwhile, I continued doing other things at the foundry. I must say everyday was very exciting for me. Going to the foundry was like having an adventure everyday, and adventure it was.

SEEING ANGELS THROUGH PA'S EYES.

It was now the beginning of February. We found out that my father-in-law was dying. I went to the foundry and told Lynn that I had to take a leave so I could spend time in town with Bud's parents. I felt bad because I had only been with Lynn for a month, but she understood. She said, "Family first, Joy." And she was right.

My father-in-law was a quiet and gentle man. He never spoke a word the whole time that I knew him. He had his voice box removed years before I met him. He would use a voice enhancer from time to time when someone couldn't read his lips, but he didn't like to.

When I was there I would tell him he didn't have to use it, because I can read lips pretty good.

The only time I would tell him he had to use his talking device was when I was taking him somewhere. One time we were going to get some lumber and he was talking away and telling me where to turn without his device and I missed the turn.
I looked at him and said is that where you wanted me to turn? He laughed and nodded his head yes. Then with his device he said, "I forgot you couldn't here me could you?"
   I laughed and said; "No and I can't read lips while I'm driving either!"

One night after Bud's sister called us to say that Pa was getting worse we went into town. Pa was lying on the couch when we arrived. He kept saying, **"I'm going home!"**

   Bud's Mom would say, "You <u>are</u> home."

Then he would smile and say, "No, _**Home!**_" And point to the ceiling.
Everyone knew what that meant, but nobody wanted to admit that he was preparing to die.

  Then Pa said, "There is a lady here."
We asked who it was and he said it was his Mother.
   The conversation went on like this for a long time. But no matter what anyone said to him he would just lay there and smile.
As Bud and I were walking to the car I said to him, "Your dad wants to go home."
   Bud replied quietly, "I know."
   I wanted so badly to tell him about the people that I saw going to heaven. I wanted to ease his pain, but the words just wouldn't come.

HE WANTED TO DIE AT HOME

I went into town every day to be with Buds parents. It turned out to be an experience of a lifetime. For two weeks it was an emotional roller-coaster ride. One-minute Pa would be at death's door and the next he would be sitting at the kitchen table saying, "I'm hungry."

When I arrived one morning, Terri, Bud's niece said, "It doesn't look good." She is a nurse's aide and had been caring for him. "He barely has a heartbeat and I can't get a blood pressure reading."

I walked over by the bed and sat down next to him. As I reached down and stroked his hair, Pa looked at me and smiled. I asked him how he was feeling?

"Great!" he said, "I'm going home, you know."

I smiled at him and said, "Yes, I know and I'm going to miss you."

He reached over and held on to my hand while he stared at the ceiling with a smile. Suddenly his eyes got as big as half-dollars. They were still fixed on the ceiling. I looked up but saw nothing. He seemed to be talking to someone. I don't think I had ever seen him smile like that or have that kind of look of indescribable happiness in his eyes.

Mom had joined us and she said, "He has been doing that all night long.
He has been real antsy."

I watched him closely and said, "He is talking to someone. Maybe they are preparing him."
Just then Pa looked at me and said,
"They are coming to get me."
NOW?" I said with surprise in my voice.

He calmly shrugged his shoulders and smiled. Later he surprised us all by getting up to go to the bathroom on his own. Then he sat at the table and said that he wanted to eat.

But by the next day he was worse again. I told Ma that I would give her a break and sit with him for awhile. As I was sitting in a chair that was facing the wall, Pa was sleeping. I was reading a book when all of a sudden something caught my eye. I looked up and saw sparkles coming down from the ceiling. It looked like gold dust falling over Pa. I don't know how long I watched this. I was in awe. There was no sun that day and the curtains were closed. I swore if I would have reached out, I could have caught some and held it in my hands. It was that clear. I knew this was sent from heaven. I sat there with my mouth open thinking, *gold dust from heaven. How cool.*

I wanted to call out to everyone that was in the kitchen but I was afraid that if I did it would disappear.

When it stopped I went into the kitchen and said with excitement,
"You guys are never going to believe this, but there was gold dust falling from the ceiling and down on Pa. Isn't that cool?"
Everyone looked at me like I had just lost my mind. Then Bud's sister, MaryJo said, "I wouldn't doubt it. If you said you saw it, than you probably did. After all, anyone who has seen an Angel probably can see all kinds of things."
I walked out of the room and went back to sit by Pa. As I sat there I said thanks to God for letting me see such a beautiful thing.
I waited for more but there was none.
When Pa woke up he called everybody around him. He looked at all of us, then

made the sign of the cross to each person,
MaryJo said, "Are you blessing us?"

Pa said, "Yes"

Then she laughed and said, "What, do you
think you are a saint?"

Pa looked at her, never more sincere and
serious. "Yes I am!" He stated.

He meant every word that was coming out
of his mouth. I felt a shiver run through my
body. His words were silent but his message
had as much impact as if an atomic bomb
had just gone off inside my head. I have
never seen him more sincere. Than he
wanted us to say the rosary with him and we
did.

I was kneeling by the bed after we said the
rosary. I looked at him and asked,
"What did you see?"

Pa's face lit up, he leaned over as if he was
going to whisper something to me but
changed his mind. I think he forgot that he
didn't have a voice box.

Then he said, "I got a peek, a peek of the other side. "With excitement I said, "You did? What was it like?"

He leaned back, his face glowing again. It was as if he was reliving the vision he had seen. Then he said, "Awesome, just awesome." At this point his face was a picture of total ecstasy.

Mom came in to sit with him and she was telling him it was ok for him to go.

They had their hands on each other's faces. They were always touching each other and holding hands. They were so in love with each other that it filled the room. Pa then said to her, "I want you to go with me."

She laughed and said, "You know I would if I could."

Once more, he said, "I don't want to leave you. I want you to come with me."

Again she laughed through her tears and said "Let's go!"

As I stood there and watched, my heart was breaking to see such a love between the two of them, yet seeing them being pulled apart. I had to walk away. I went into the kitchen and cried.

This went on every day, Pa asking mom to go with him. I will say it was just as hard hearing those words the hundredth time as it was the first.

One day I was tired so I laid down next to Pa. I was watching him sleep and then fell asleep also. I woke to something tickling my nose. I thought it was a fly, so without opening my eyes, I shooed it away. Again something touched my nose. I opened my eyes as I was shooing it away, and there was Pa with a big smile on his face. He was tickling the end of my nose with the blanket.

"So you're awake now, huh?" I asked.
He smiled at me and said, "Yes and now you are too!" We both laughed.

Then Pa looked at me and said, "Did you know you have an Angel standing behind you?"
I smiled and nodded. "Yes, isn't he beautiful?" Pa smiled and agreed.
"His name is Gabriel" I told him.
Again Pa smiled and nodded his head yes. If I had ever had any doubts about Gabriel being at my side, they vanished at that very moment. Then Pa started looking around the room like he was seeing something. Over the next few days he would tell us that there were people in the room but we could not see them. Mom was playing 20 questions with him trying to figure out who they were. As we would guess a name of someone in the family that had passed on, Pa would just shrug his shoulders and smile.

It also became normal to see him talking to (The beautiful woman) as he would call her. He would say, "The beautiful woman is coming" and point to the ceiling. Then he would go into a trance-like state where his eyes were fixed and he would start to glow. He would smile from ear to ear then he would talk to someone, but we could never make out what he was saying. When she would leave he would return back to normal and smile.

We would ask him who it was that he was seeing and he would point to the statue of the Blessed Mother Mary. I asked him, "Is it Mother Mary that you see?" And he said, "Yes."

One day Lisa, (one of Bud's daughters) and I were sitting on the bed talking to Pa, when his eyes went up to the ceiling and his head bent back and he started to glow again.

I said to Lisa, "Look he is seeing Mother Mary again."

We watched as he talked to her. We looked at the ceiling, wishing we too could see her. When he was done he looked at us and I said, "What did she say?"

He was so excited to tell us what she had said to him, that he was talking too fast and we couldn't' read his lips.
"Pa, I can't read your lips when you talk that fast."
He smiled and started talking slower this time but not by much. I found myself trying so hard to understand him but I could not.
Finally I said, "Its ok Pa, maybe we are not supposed to know what you saw."
He just smiled and looked back at the ceiling. He was very content. As he lay there he kept touching the hole in his throat, as if it were going to go away.

At one point he said, "I can talk, can you hear me?"

I said, "No."

"I can talk there," he said and pointed to the heavens. I just smiled and said, "That is so cool Pa."

When he was talking to the spirits around him, I do believe he could hear himself talk.

THE DAY
HEAVEN'S GATES OPENED

The day was finally here. I knew it as soon as I walked into the house. There was a sweet aroma in the air, like roses. I looked around to see if anyone had brought flowers over, but no one had. Then it dawned on me. Pa was going home today. My heart felt sad because I would miss him, but happy for him because he was going to a much better place. I kept telling myself, *What could be better than seeing Jesus and being in heaven.*

Part of me wished that I could go with him. I stood by the door and took a deep breath, then I thought of when my Grandma died. She was in a coma. I was told about the special rosary that you sing for the dyeing called The Chaplet of Mercy. It was told to Sister Faustina by Jesus and he promised her that if people sing this

rosary or as a prayer in the presents of the dyeing that no matter if they are the most hardened criminal or the mildest sinner that they will receive special graces with God apon there death. (Anyone can say this prayer).
I sung the rosary to Grandma one day. And then asked God to give me a sign that it worked. And that night while in her coma she sung with a smile on her glowing face all night long and continued to do so for two nights in a row.
I told my Mom that she was hearing and singing with the angels. The doctors had said it couldn't be, because she was in a coma. But what do they know? We know what we saw and heard. I knew that my question to God was answered and I thanked him for this conformation. She passed into God's hands on the third day.

I pulled myself together and walked to Pa's bedside. Mom said that he was in good spirits but was sleeping a lot. He would wake up and talk then go back to sleep.

Pa was not taking any pain medications because he was not in any pain. There was nothing wrong with him except that he was just ready to go home. All of us spent the day sitting around his bed. He would wake up and ask us to pray the rosary and we would. I thought to myself, *I'm not sure why he would want us to say the rosary for him. He has already seen Mother Mary and a peek of heaven.* Then it dawned on me: *He didn't want us to pray for him, he wanted us to say the prayers for each other and for ourselves. God and Pa knew we all could use more prayers.*

The day had come. The hour was here. Pa was going home. I sat next to him for a couple of minutes and held his hand. He opened his eyes and smiled at me.

"Are you going to leave us now?" I asked.

"Yes." He said.

"Could you do me one last favor?" I asked.

He smiled and said, "Sure what?" The tears were rolling down my cheeks.
My heart was breaking.

"Well," I managed to say, "When you get to heaven and you see Jesus, will you put in a good word for me?"

Pa looked at me and smiled. Then he reached up to my face and wiped the tears off my cheek with his thumb. He then touched my forehead with his thumb and my tear. He then made the sign of the cross on my forehead. I'm not sure why but I said, "Amen" when he did this.

I accepted the blessing he had just given me with my heart and soul. Then he patted my hand and said that he would give Jesus my message.

"I love you Pa," I said, then gave him a kiss.

"I love you too," he replied then he closed his eyes. I went to the kitchen and told Mom that I thought it was time.
She went and sat next to him. She took his hand then leaned in and gave him a kiss, and told him that she loved him then said goodbye. That is the moment Pa left us and went home.

MORE GOLD DUST

The next morning we went to Ma's house to prepare for the funeral. We were all sitting at the kitchen table when Ma said, "You're not going to believe this."

I spoke up and said, "I will. What?"

She continued, "Well last night I was lying in bed and I kept seeing something shinning, so I got up and looked out of the windows thinking that maybe there was a light coming in from outside. But there wasn't. All the curtains were closed. Then something caught my eye. I looked up and here were pillars of gold dust coming from the ceiling and falling right where Pa had slept.
It was the strangest thing."

Then Bud's nephew said, "I saw it too.
I was lying on the floor trying to sleep and something caught my eye. I looked into the room where Grandma was and I saw the pillar of gold dust falling.

I wasn't going to say anything. I figured everyone would think I was nuts."

I laughed and said, "Ma, that is Pa's way of telling you he made it to heaven."

A couple of days after the funeral, things had finally caught up with me. I was exhausted so I laid on the couch to catch a few winks. I started to drift off to sleep. When all of a sudden, I felt something touching the end of my nose. I thought to myself, "darn fly." Then I rubbed the end of my nose. I started to drift off again, the same thing happened. I opened my eyes to see what was tickling my nose. But there was nothing there. I remembered when I had laid down next to Pa and he had tickled my nose with the blanket. I laughed out loud and said, "Ok Pa, I'm awake now." After I had said this, the tickling stopped and I fell asleep with no problem.

Days later, Buds eight-year-old niece Becky,

told her Mom that she had a dream about great-grandpa. "He was talking to me," she said. "I could hear him. He didn't have to use that thing that helped him talk either. "We all sat around the kitchen table, reminiscing about how Pa kept acting like he could talk. And how he acted like we all could hear him.

Then Kathy spoke up and told us what had happened to her on her birthday. She explained how her and Pa loved to save pennies. And on her birthday she found penny's everywhere she went, in a doorway or on a bench and on the floor at a restaurant. Kathy said Pa was sending her pennies from heaven to let her know he was with her on her birthday. She said that she knew that they were from her grandpa because every time she would see one he would come into her mind.

STRANGE THINGS STARTED HAPPENING

It was the middle of April. I decided it was time to start Gabriel's hands. I needed to make an armature for them. I looked at my hands to see if they would work, but they were too big. I went to everyone in the house, looking for a model for the frame. No one's hands would work. They were all too big. Then Tyler, (my youngest) came up to me and said, "Will mine work?" I looked at his tiny hands and said, "You know, I think they will." I figured after the clay was on the wire they would be just about the right size.

I took the armature wire and measured it to his fingers and the palms of his hands. Tyler's little hand turned out to be a perfect model for the armature for Gabriel's hands. I covered one of the wire hands with clay.

Then, without devoting a lot attention to it.
I worked on the hand while watching TV.
After only a short while, I looked down at
the hand and it was already done. I couldn't
believe it. Then I looked at the clock on the
wall. It had only been two hours and this
hand was done except for the fingernails.

I showed Bud and said isn't this weird? He
just looked at me and shook his head. He
had no clue as to what I was talking about.
So I said, "Look, this hand is done." "How
did you do that so fast?" he asked. I didn't,
I said. Someone must be working through
me. There is no way I could do this. I
wasn't even paying attention to what I was
doing. I was just sitting there, watching TV
and pushing the clay onto the wires. At least
I thought so. And when I looked down,
there it was. His hand was done. We stared
at each other for a moment. I started
laughing and said, isn't this neat? Weird,
but neat? Bud didn't say a word he just

shook his head. I started on the other hand and the same thing happened. Within two hours of starting it, it was also done. All I had to do is add the fingernails. I was so excited. I couldn't wait to attach Gabriel's hands to him.

When I attached the left one, it was like magic. I could feel the energy coming from it and running up my arms. Then I attached the right hand. Instantly I could sense something wrong. There was no energy. Frustrated, I sat with Gabriel's clay hand in mine and studied it. I could not see what was wrong. I closed my eyes, focusing first on Gabriel, then on his hands. Still I could not see what was wrong with it. I put the hand on anyway to see what he looked like. I started to walk away from the statue; I was going to sit on the couch so I could study the statue from a distance. By the time I reached the couch, I heard a thud.

The noise stunned me because it was so loud. I thought the whole statue had fallen over. I turned around to find his hand on the pallet by his foot. It had fallen off. I walked over to put the hand back on. I thought, maybe I wasn't using enough clay to hold it on. So I put more clay around his wrist this time. Again as I walked away and started to sit down I heard another thud. I looked back only to find his hand lying on the pallet again. Bud asked, "why is the one staying on but the other isn't?" I had the same question running through my head. When I finally answered him I said, "Well there is something wrong with his hand. He doesn't like it." Bud looked at me and said, "Yeah right." Yes, I said I know I'm right! There isn't any energy in that one. Something is wrong with it. I turned and looked at Bud after I said this, and he had that "she's lost it," look on his face again. This went on for days. I would put the hand on and it would fall right back off. Finally I sat the hand aside and stopped trying to put it on.

EASTER SUNDAY

When we woke up Easter Sunday, Bud said, "Joy, are you going to put Gabriel's hand on him? After all, you don't want the grand children to see an Angel with only one hand. It might scare them." We both laughed. I said, "I told you he doesn't like this hand and he wont leave it on. And if I put it on, it will only fall off again.
" Give it to me he said, I will put it on him. You're just not doing it right." I smiled and handed him the clay hand. While Bud was putting the hand on, I put my arm around the statue's shoulders and said, "Gabriel please leave your hand on today, at least until everyone leaves. Ok?" Bud looked at me and said, "Joy, you have to stop talking to

this statue, people are going to think your nuts." I laughed and said, "So, what do I care? Some people already do."

 After everyone arrived, I was sitting on the couch talking when I noticed Heaven Alisa, one of the grandchildren. She was squatting on the floor looking up at Gabriel. She was only two years old and very mischievous. She was looking at all the tools I was using to sculpt with. She had a look on her face like "I can do this." She picked up a tool, looked up at Gabriel and then she looked back at the tool in her hand. She sat there for a few minutes. You could tell her little mind was at work. Shamber, her mom, was going to say something to her and I said, "No don't say anything just watch, Gabriel won't let anything happen." Shamber said, "boy you have a lot of faith in that angel, don't you?" I laughed and said, "Just watch." We watched her as she stared up at Gabriel. She became very still.

Then all of a sudden she laid the tool down, stood up and started to walk away.

She would stop every step or so and turn around to stare at Gabriel. It was as if he was talking to her. She did not go back over by him again, she sat on the couch and stared at him for a long, long time. She was a perfect little angel the rest of the day.

After everyone left, Bud and I were sitting on the couch relaxing when all of a sudden we heard a thud. I started laughing and Bud asked, "What was that?" Well, I said if you look over at the statue, his hand is probably laying on the pallet. We both looked and I was right once again. Through my laughter I said, "See he did as I asked him to. He left his hand on until everyone was gone." Bud just shook his head.

As the days passed, I kept working on his right hand. Actually, I just kept looking at it and then at the left to see if I could figure out what was wrong with this hand. I just couldn't seem to see what it is.

The next day my friend Ella came over and I told her what was going on with the hand. She said, "Let me look at it." We walked up to Gabriel and looked at the hand that was on and then at the right one. All of a sudden it came to me and at the same time we both said, "There is no lifeline in this one." There was one in the left one but not in the right hand. I could not believe that I didn't see something so obvious. I grabbed one of my tools and put his lifeline in it and then I put the hand on him. As I was attaching the hand, I could feel the electricity running through my hands like it had when I attached the left one. I knew that the problem was solved. Later that night Bud asked me how I had got Gabriel's hand to stay on. I said, "You're not going to believe this, but it was something so simple.

I forgot to put his lifeline in it."
I remembered the lifeline in the other hand
but forgot about this one. I don't know how
I missed it?

   Bud said "Joy that's just a little line. It is
not a big deal." I said, little line yes but a
very important line.   Without it you have no
life. Bud looked at me, then said, "You are
very strange, Joy Marie." Laughing I said, I
might be strange but Gabriel will now have
two hands that stay on.

   The hand never fell off again.

MAY 4,1997
KENTUCKY DERBY DAY

Every year, we have a Kentucky Derby Party at our home. Everyone was buzzing around getting ready for the party. I was in the house alone, cleaning. As I was tidying around the almost completed statue of Gabriel, I put my hand on his face and said, "Gabriel, is this really happening or have I really lost my mind?" Not waiting for a reply, I continued, "I don't doubt that you are real, I just can't understand why you picked me to do something so special. But I do thank you for believing in me. And with God and your help, I will do my best for you both." I felt a wonderful sense of peace come over me.

Going back to cleaning, I started scrubbing the kitchen floor, all the time thinking about everything that had happened with Gabriel so far. Not surprisingly this was something that I had found myself thinking about a lot. So much had happened and I was wondering how much of this was a coincidence or not.

Instantly, I heard the words in my head.

"There are no coincidences only reality."

Just then a song came on the radio that caught my attention and touched a spot in my soul. I felt as if it had been written for me. I stopped my work and listened to the meaningful words:

You were dreaming on a park bench about a broad highway somewhere.

When the music from the Caroline seemed to hurl your heart out there.

To an angel bending down to wrap you in his warmest coat.

And you ask what am I not doing?

He said your voice can not come in.

But in time you will move mountains.

It will come through your hands.

The lyrics ran through me as I was sitting on my knees on the floor. I felt as if I had been hit on the head with something. Everything in the room seemed to be shaking. I could feel the tears coming on. It seemed as if once again my questions were answered.

I walked over to Gabriel and said I will never doubt you again. I grabbed the phone and called my friend Terri Slomski and asked her if she had ever heard the song. She hadn't and then asked me what the name of it was. I told her that I didn't know and that was why I was calling her.

Terri said, "I have been meaning to tell you that you should see the movie, *Michael.* It is about an Angel."

"Yeah, I heard about it, but I don't have any interest in seeing it to be honest. From what I've heard it would irritate me to see an Angel portrayed like that one is.

That movie portrays an Angel like a
smoking, womanizing man would act, not
like an Angel really is." We talked about
this a little more then she said; "Good luck
on finding that song. See yah later."
    As people arrived they would come into
the house to see the statue of Gabriel.
Most of them were in awe. Their reactions
were exactly what I needed to see. It was
wonderful to see so many people touched by
something that came from God and Gabriel's
hand through mine. Everybody made the
comment about the movie *Michael*. Some
told me I should see it, while others said not
to. I told them the same thing that I had told
Terri, that I have no desire to see it.

    As the weeks went on I looked and
listened for that song to be played again. I
would stop at music stores and ask if they
knew what the name of it was. I would even
sing it to the people who worked there but

they had never heard it before. Then one day the kids and I went to rent a video. While I was there I saw the movie *Michael* on the shelf. I picked it up, then put it down, then picked it up again. The next thing I knew I had rented it. Bud said, "I thought you didn't want to see it." I said "me too but for some reason I'm renting it. I figure there must be a message in here for me or something."

As we watched it, I found myself bored and disturbed by some of the scenes. I just couldn't imagine Gabriel ever acting that way. "If this is the way Hollywood and people think heaven is," I told Bud, "It's no wonder this world is such a sad place to live in."

I left the room in the middle of the movie to go into the kitchen and started washing up a few dishes. When it was over, I heard the music begin.

Tyler got up to rewind the movie. I told him, "Let it play, I want to hear that song." I walked into the family room and said to Bud, "This is the song I have been looking for!"

I must have rewound and played that song ten times. I went to the store the next day and bought the sound track. The name of the song was *Through your hands* by Don Henley. Once again I thought ask and you shall receive even when you are looking for something as simple as a song. The answer is always right in front of you.

WORKING ON THE WINGS

For the next three weeks I worked on making Gabriel's wings. I rolled out clay and cut pieces to look like feathers. Then I took a tool and scoured the clay to make marks in it so it would look like individual feathers. This was very tedious and time-consuming work, but just as Gabriel had told me. I only had to close my eyes and the sight and feel of his wings were vividly clear to me. When I would find myself getting tired I would hear the song, Through your hands or I believe I can fly and it would pick my spirit back up and I would continue working.

As I added the feathers, I kept trying to bend the wire in the wings so they would dip in. I knew how they were supposed to look, but the wire would not cooperate. I needed them to look as if he was getting ready to

fly. He had to look as if he was ready to
pick us up if we called upon him. I had
already placed Gabriel's hands as if he was
reaching for someone. I needed him to look
this way so that when the firemen or other
people looked at Gabriel they would get the
impression that he was reaching out to them
and ready to help at any moment.

One night Bud said to me, "You need to
bend the wings more." How? I answered.
I have tried but I just can't do it." Bud came
over and tried to bend the armature wire, but
he had no luck either. I told him that I
would worry about it later. For the time
being I just wanted to get the feathers on the
wings. At this point the wings looked as if
they were going straight up in the air.

Finally the feathers were complete.
Gabriel was finished. Bud asked me if I was
going to ask our priest to come and bless
Gabriel before I took him up to the foundry.

I was worried about what he would think.
Maybe he would think I was Crazy?
These thoughts kept running through my
mind. I walked up to Gabriel's statue and
said, "Is this what you would like?"

I felt a sense of peace come over me.
So on Sunday I asked Father if he would
come to the house and bless a statue that I
made, before I took it to the foundry.
He asked if I would bring the statue to the
church so that he could bless it there. I told
him it was way too big and I didn't want to
take a chance on driving him that far in case
something happened to it.

He said he would be glad to do it for me
and he would be at the house on Monday
morning. He never asked any questions
about what kind of statue it was.
I was relieved.

MONDAY MORNING

Before Father arrived my stomach was in knots, I was so nervous and troubled thoughts filled my mind. *How am I going to tell a man of God about how an Angel named Gabriel came to me? And how he told me to make a statue of him, then give it away?*
After all most people didn't believe me, why should he? (I heard a different priest talking once about how a lady told him that she seen Mother Mary, and how he thought she was totally crazy) The last thing I wanted was for my priest to think this way of me, because I am far from crazy. It even entered my mind that, *Father is going to suggest to Bud to have me committed… and he sad thing is Bud would go along with him!* Then I began to hope that Father wouldn't ask any questions. *Maybe he would just bless Gabriel and that would be that.*

*I wouldn't have to explain myself at all.
Or maybe I could just tell him that this was
something I just wanted to do. Finally, I
decided that if he did ask. I would tell him
the truth. I would tell him everything.
Well almost everything.*

I found myself getting even more and
more nervous, so I walked over to Gabriel's
statue and said, "You are going to have to
help me explain this to Father. I really
would appreciate it if you could give me the
words to use. Better yet, you could talk for
me. I just don't know how I am going to tell
him about you."

Once again, the feeling of total calm came
over me and I knew things were going to be
all right. It was at that moment when I saw
Father drive it to the driveway. I went out to
meet him and thanked him for coming to do
this for me.

I showed him in and pointed him in the
direction of Gabriel.

Father looked at Gabriel. And said, "Wow, he is big isn't he? Now I know why you couldn't bring him to the church for me to bless him there!"

He walked over and sat down in the chair that was at my desk in front of Gabriel. He leaned forward and started to look Gabriel over. "You did a nice job on this Angel." He said.

"Thank you. It's the first time I have ever tried anything like this."

Then I thought, *So far so good!*

Father looked at me and said, "Ok Joy, tell me why you made this statue, and don't tell me he came to you as a vision."

I winced and thought, *here we go, Gabriel, this is where I need you to help me.* I smiled and looked at Father, "Ok I will tell you… but remember you asked. He came to me in a dream."

Father watched me as I spoke, I continued.

"Well you could call it a dream but I say it was a vision because it was as real to me as looking at you and talking to you right now. So you can call it what ever you would like."

Father continued looking at me and listening to what I was saying. I told him how Gabriel came to me two nights in a row and how he had me touch his gown and his feathers. I explained how he had said he would help people all over the world and that I didn't know how he was going to do this yet. But he said that it was all taken care of. I finished by saying, "And he told me his name was Gabriel."

When I said this, Father's eyes went back to the statue. While I told him the rest of the story Father never took his eyes from Gabriel. I didn't go into very much detail. I just told him what I thought he needed to hear.

"You know Joy," Father said, he would look nice even if he didn't have any wings."

I nodded. "But I like his wings." I said.
"Oh, I do too. I just mean he looks very angelic and he would look like an Angel even if he didn't have any wings."

"Oh, I though you meant that you didn't like them."

Father assured me that, that wasn't the case, only that he really didn't need them to look like an Angel."

"You know what, Father? I never even thought of that. I had never thought about trying to make him look angelic. I just made the statue look like Gabriel."

Any doubts that might have been following me around during the past months left. I realized Gabriel's statue did look angelic. I had just seen it through the eyes of someone else.

My emotions were running away with me again and I fought back the tears.
Father said, "Ok, I will bless him now."

We said a prayer together then Father said a prayer. I can not remember all the words but they were the words that Gabriel used about helping people. Then Father sprinkled him with Holy Water. We said another prayer together and he was done.

Later on that night, Bud and I were talking. I was sitting on the floor with my back to Gabriel's statue, while Bud was on the couch across the room facing him. I was telling him that I was planning to take the statue up to the foundry the next day. "Won't it be strange not to have Gabriel here when you get home?" I asked.

Bud said, "Yes, so why don't you just leave him here and forget about giving him away?"

I laughed and said, "Because I don't think Gabriel would appreciate it if all of a sudden I became selfish and he couldn't help all the people who need him."

I knew where Bud was coming from.
I didn't want the statue to leave either.
I kept thinking how empty this room would
feel without Gabriel in it, even though I told
Bud that I was excited about getting him
completed and getting him to the firemen.

We sat in silence for a while when all of a
sudden I heard Bud exclaim, "Joy, look
behind you!" The sound of his voice scared
me.

"No, way." I said. Tell me what's wrong?

"Look, look at Gabriel!" Bud insisted.

"NO!" I said, his voice was scarring me.
I was staring at Bud but he was looking past
me at Gabriel. He had a look of total
disbelief on his face.

"He's not walking or reaching out to touch
me is he?" I laughed nervously. I could
hear my heart beating. Bud didn't say
anything. The look on his face was too
much. I turned around not knowing what I
was going to see. When I looked at Gabriel,

I was completely amazed as well.
It was breathtaking.
His wings were slowly coming down...
both at the same time.
This was very strange because the wires in
the wings were not attached to each other.
I could understand if one fell but not both
at the same time. They started to fold just a
little. Right where I knew they were
supposed to. I said, "OH MY!
Father jinxed Gabriel's wings! He said he
didn't need them and now Gabriel is
shedding them."
Just then they stopped moving. We stared
in total disbelief of what we had just
witnessed. It was as if someone was putting
the wings the way they were supposed to be.
Bud and I looked at each other and started
laughing. "Wow!" I gasped. "Now that is
the way that Gabriel wanted them. That's
what I was trying to tell you before."

We both laughed again. I said, "I'm glad that Father didn't jinx him after all. He had me worried for a moment there."

I looked at Gabriel and said, "Thank you."
"Why did you say that?" Bud asked.
"Because," I said, "You finally got to see the kind of things that happen with Gabriel. You know, like the things I have been trying to tell you about, and you keep telling me that you're worried about me."
We both laughed. Bud said, "OK, I'll admit it - that was strange."
"Not really," I smiled. "I told you that the wings were not right. And now you saw for yourself how Gabriel can fix things."

GABRIEL IS READY TO GO

I told Lynn that Gabriel was done. She told me to cut off his wings and bring them up to the foundry first. This way, she said, your Angel will be easier to haul up here. We will have to do this anyway. Lynn continued, so go ahead and do that at home.

This was hard for me to do emotionally, but I knew that it had to be done. I first cut off the right wing with a hacksaw. Also I was afraid that once it was off, I would drop it and mess up the clay feathers. I was praying hard that everything would go smoothly. As was becoming normal, my emotions went from fear to calm. I kept telling myself that Gabriel would not let anything happen and that everything would be all right.

I put a big pillow in the front seat of the truck. Then I laid the wing on the pillow. I took wing up to the foundry.

Then I came back home for the left one and did the same again.

At the foundry, everyone liked the detail that I put in the wings. I was so pleased to get the approval from these people whose opinions I valued so greatly.

Lynn chose Adam to help me make the mold. (Adam was a college student Lynn had hired for the summer.) I must say I was glad that she chose Adam to help me, he is an excellent mold maker.

Adam and I started to make the rubber and painting it on the wings. This was not a fun job. We had to make sure that every centimeter was covered with the rubber and that there were no bubbles. I would mix the rubber and Adam would paint it on. When finished, the rubber had to be approximately 1 to 1 1/2 inches thick. It was a long process. After a day or so of putting rubber on the wings it was time to take Gabriel to the foundry.

The night before, I asked Bud to help me load him in the truck. He said that it was going to rain and he didn't think that was a very good idea and to wait until the next morning to load him.

Morning came and Bud was late for work so he couldn't help me. I wanted to cry. I didn't know how I was going to get Gabriel into the truck. He was too heavy for me to lift by myself, but I had little choice. After backing the truck up to the door, I went in the house and pushed the pallet with Gabriel on it over to the door.

This was as far as I could get it. I was trying to be careful so the clay wouldn't crack. I figured if I could get him on the porch then I could slowly lift one end up on the truck then the other with no problem. The more I thought about it, the more I realized I needed help. Just then my phone rang. It was Dee Smith a dear friend.

I told her what I was trying to do and she said, "Are you nuts?"

I told her, "Yeah, so why don't you come down and help me?"

"No, I can't." She replied.

Desperately, I said, "All I need you to do is lift up one end of it and help me push it into the truck."

Dee asked. "How are you going to get him up to the foundry without anyone holding onto him? I said, "He will be fine, I will just have to go really slow." After she told me that I was nuts again she came down and helped me load him. Everything went as planned with no problems.

As I drove my thoughts went back to the day when Bud and I brought home the armature. I had told the kids, "Can you imagine Gabriel standing in the back of the truck, looking forward with the wind in his face... going back to the foundry to be made into a mold?" Tyler and Autumn said that they could imagine it.

Now that day was here, 3 1/2 months later. I drove about four miles per hour. My thoughts were with every bump that I ran over. I never realized just how rough our road was, till now. When I finally reached a smooth road I was more relaxed, but still I drove slowly. I could picture Gabriel, (The real Angel), standing with a big smile in the back of the truck with the wind blowing through his hair watching over the statue. That thought made me feel good inside and I felt that I could relax, just a little. I knew that Gabriel would not let anything happen to his statue.

We made it to the foundry without any problems. The first thing I did when I arrived was look the statue over to make sure that there were no crack or damage to it. I was relieved. Everything was fine.

Everyone came out to see the statue. I waited to see their reaction. After all, they are the artists and their opinion meant the world to me. I stared at their faces. Their words were "Wow! You did a nice job," and "I can't believe there are no cracks from the ride up here." I could tell that they like him.

When Lynn came into work, she looked Gabriel over and said that I did a good job. Then she said, "Now you have to cut off his arms. This was so we could make a separate mold for them. I felt sick inside at the thought of doing this. So I asked Lynn if she could do it for me and explained to her that I just couldn't bear to cut them off. Then I told her what a hard time mentally I had cutting off his wings. I pleaded with her to do this for me. Then I explained that she had more experience doing this than I did and I didn't want to mess it up.

She laughed and said that she would.

After a day or so of preparation, Adam and I started making the rubber and painting it on the body of Gabriel. This was a long and painstaking process. Everyday we would paint on two sometimes three coats of rubber onto the clay statue. And everyday I would ask Adam, "So how many more coats until we are done with this part?"
He would smile and say, "A lot."
We both wanted to get this part over and done with. Adam was very patient with me and my questions, which I am sure, were irritating to him to some extent.

Finally, the last coat of rubber was painted on. This was a very happy day for me because I knew we were one step closer to pouring the statue. And I'm sure it was a happy day for Adam as well. We made the outside shell out of plaster. This is to keep the rubber in its proper form.

With this done, we could now open up the plaster and rubber, and take out the clay. I couldn't believe it we were finally done with this part.

As we pulled the mold apart to take out the clay, I felt like a mother that was going to give birth, and waiting to see what her child looked like. I was nervous and praying that nothing had gone wrong.

We started with the wings and arms. They were perfect. Nothing had gone wrong with them.

Now it was time to take apart the plaster on the body part of Gabriel. We pulled and pushed for what seemed like forever. For some reason some of the rubber was sticking to the plaster. Every now and then John would come over and give Adam hints on what was holding us up. Finally we did it.

We opened up the plaster mold. Now it was time to take out the clay statue from the rubber. As we were pulling back part of the rubber mold, the clay Gabriel had fallen into my arms like a lifeless body. I wanted to cry. I felt as if somehow I had hurt Gabriel. Adam said, "Come and help me with this mold it's heavy."

I wasn't able to move. All I could do is hold the clay statue and try to hold my emotions in. Again Adam said, "Joy, drop the clay and come and help me."

"I can't." I said, I didn't know why but I just couldn't let go of the sculpture.

"Joy just let him drop to the floor!" Adam insisted.

I held back my tears and said, "But if I drop him, I might hurt him." As I heard myself say these words I thought, *Joy, it is only clay, not Gabriel.*

Just then someone came over to help Adam with the mold. I looked at Adam and said, "I am so sorry."

He smiled at me and said, "that's ok, but you're going to have to put him down sooner or later."

"I know," I admitted. "Would you help me lay him down on his back so he won't break apart?"

Adam laughed and said, "What are you going to do when you have to take the clay off of the armature? The thought of doing this sent a cold chill down my spine.
I looked at him and said, "I can't do that. Someone else will have to."

We leaned Gabriel backwards till he was lying on his back on the floor. He broke at the waistline. I stood over him and stared. Adam was standing beside me. All of a sudden we heard this weird noise. I asked Adam what it was but he didn't know. The noise was coming from the floor. It was the clay statue of Gabriel. We both looked at each other.

Adam said jokingly, "Look Joy, you hurt him." I knew he was messing around with me. Just then John was walking by. He stopped and looked at Gabriel and said, "Wow that's weird."

I asked, "Is this what sculptures normally do when you take them out of a mold?" I was praying he would say yes, but instead, John said, "I have never heard anything like it before. That is really weird," then he walked away.

I looked at Adam, then back at the clay statue. The noise was getting weaker and weaker until finally it stopped. Then Adam said, "You killed him Joy," with laughter in his voice.

Sandy walked over and said, "It's ok Joy, that is just Gabriel's spirit leaving the clay and going into the mold."

Adam shook his head and walked away. He probably thought I had really lost my mind.

 He didn't understand that this was much more to me than a hunk of clay. Of course, I didn't really expect him to understand either.

 What Sandy had said made me feel much better. I looked at her and thanked her for her kind words of comfort. Now I could go on with my job.

 I had to take all of the clay out of the molds and wash them. Then I poured hot wax into them to get the small amounts of clay out of the indents.

 I just had to see how Gabriel's face turned out. So I poured the wax in the face part and waited for it to dry. I was able to pull it out in one piece. I sat on the floor staring at this beautiful wax face that was in my hands. I started getting the feeling that I had when I was with Gabriel. My hands felt energized again. I knew in my heart that the firemen and rescue workers would just love him. I also knew that Gabriel would finally be

where he wanted to be. I felt as if I was glowing, I was so full of love.
His face was beautiful, peaceful, full of understanding and comfort. I was so excited with the results that I had to show everyone the wax face. I couldn't wait to pour him in the Forton, and get him put together.

The day was finally here. The molds were cleaned and we were ready to start pouring the Forton. I was very excited. I kept telling myself that soon I would get to see Gabriel in one piece again. I mixed the Forton and spread it into the molds.
This took some time but not as long as the mold making did.
The moment was here, at last. Adam and I pulled the rubber off of the Forton. And for the first time I was able to see what Gabriel was going to look like. He was beautiful.
I stared at his face and tried to picture Gabriel's face that I had made in the clay.

Something looked different. I didn't know what it was. I was staring at his eyes they seemed to be smiling at me. I didn't notice this in the clay. Then I stared at his lips. They also seemed to have more of a smile on them than I had remembered.

I didn't say anything about this to anyone. I just thought it was my imagination. Lynn came in to see how Gabriel looked and she said, "You know his eyes seem different and so do his lips. They seem to be smiling more."

I looked at her and said, "Yeah I thought so too."

"Joy, she said nothing would shock me when it comes to your Angel."

I felt so proud. Then I thought, *"what if he doesn't look all that good? What if I am the only one who thinks he is beautiful?"* I came to the conclusion that I really didn't care what others thought about how he looked, he looked wonderful to me and that was all that mattered.

I stood there thinking again about what had taken place in the last few months. In my mind's eye I could see Gabriel with a big smile on his face. Then I heard his voice saying, *"Well done."* This was all the conformation that I needed.

Adam and I gathered all the pieces of Gabriel and started putting him together. Thad did all the welding for us. He had to weld Rebar that was in the wings to a steel post that ran down the center of Gabriel, to a steel plate in the base.

Gabriel went together like a hand in a glove. There were no problems and we were down to the wire. I had only three days left to go before Community Day and there was still a lot of work left to do on the statue.

I had to smooth out all of the seams and fix anything that needed fixing. I worked on this for two days. Finally I was satisfied with the way everything looked.

I was talking to Adam about painting Gabriel. I wanted to paint him in color the way that I saw him when he came to me. Adam kept telling me that I should do the whole statue in white. He said, "Joy picture this in your mind; a beautiful blue sky with Gabriel all in white, don't you think that would be neat? It would look like an Angel coming down from heaven."

"Yeah, but what if the firemen have him on the ground and there is snow all around him? Then you wouldn't be able to see him. If he was in color at least you could see the details of his gown and his feathers."

"Well," Adam said, "You could paint him anyway that you would like, I just think he would look good in all white."

"You're probably right," I admitted,
"But I will have to think about this."
When I went home that night I asked Bud
what he thought and he also said,
"All white," In my mind I just couldn't see
Gabriel that way. I could only see him in
color with his silky gown and his gold belt
and sandals.

I could see his brown skin that glistened
and hair that flowed like a river with a
golden sunset dancing on the water. And
those big beautiful blue eyes that would just
melt your soul.

Bud reminded me that I only had one more
day to get him painted and I knew that I
would never find the paint that I needed.
So I went with Bud and Adam's opinion and
painted him all white. While I was painting
the statue, I kept apologizing to Gabriel
about painting him all one color. But it
worked out just fine in the end.

I put the final touches on him at the end of the day.

I think everyone was surprised that I didn't have to work on him late into the night.

I was done by 7.00 PM Friday night.

When he was completed, I put my hand on the statue's shoulders and looked him in his eyes and said, "Well Gabriel, tomorrow you will be able to start the healing, just like you said you would. I do hope the firemen know just how lucky they are to have you."

I was excited for our firemen to get Gabriel, but my mind kept going to all the other police and rescue workers that I saw that night in January. My heart hurt for them because I knew that they also needed Gabriel and I didn't know how I was going to get him to them. I knew that there was no way that I could make a statue for everyone of the departments. The cost would be phenomenal. Then I heard Gabriel's voice saying, *"It is all taken care of. In time this will also come."* At this moment I let the feeling of sadness go and concentrated on what tomorrow would bring.

SATURDAY JULY 12,1997
COMMUNITY DAY

The day had finally arrived. I woke up to my husband's voice saying "Joy, get up. You have an Angel to give away today."
I smiled and said, "I know." I laid there thinking that it had been five months and nineteen days since Gabriel came to me on that cold January night. And how wild it had been and how everything came together. I wondered how the firemen were going to react? Would they think I was some kind of crazy woman? What would they say? Then once again a wave of sadness came over me

because I didn't do anything for all of the other people that were involved in the crash. I closed my eyes for a moment and asked Gabriel to give me a sign that everything would work out. Even thought the day before he had already told me that it would. I just wanted to be reassured one more time.

I could see his beautiful face and that beautiful smile. Then once again I heard Gabriel saying,

"Don't worry, everything is taken care of."

"But Gabriel, what about the other firemen, the police and their families and all the others? What can I do for them?"
Again he smiled and said,

"In time you will know, it is all taken care of."

Bud began talking to me and I lost my concentration. I asked Bud to repeat what he had said. He told me that he had bought the Alabama's *Angels Among Us* CD.

"I think we should play this when you give the firemen the Angel." I looked at him and said, "That would be a great idea." I had goose bumps at the thought of hearing that song. Then I said, "That is the song that confirmed this whole thing for me.
It might as well be the song that ends it."

The word 'end' echoed through my head. I though, *yep this is the end. It is all over as of today.* Part of me was sad to see this day come, yet another part of me was happy because the firemen would have Gabriel and he could start doing his work for them.

I got out of bed and told Bud that we had to be uptown by 11.00 A.M. Mike, (Bud's grandson) was going to tell the firemen that they were supposed to meet in the center of town after they were done with the parade.

That is when we would give Gabriel to the firemen.

Bud asked me, "What are you going to say to them?"

"I don't know. I haven't even thought about it." I laughed, "something short and sweet."

"Well you had better get thinking about what you're going to say." He answered.

"I will know when the time comes. Thinking about it will drive me nuts and besides I would just forget anyway. So I'm not going to think about it right now. Gabriel will tell me what to say, I'm sure of that." Bud looked at me and shook his head. The phone started ringing with friends and family calling to see if I was nervous and telling me that they were coming to watch. The phone must have rang 50 times before we left. My mom called to tell me that my sisters and brothers were coming too. This made the day even more special for me.

Bud came in the house and said that it was time to go, "So you can give my Angel away." He added.

The words he had said didn't register in my head. I just said, "Good, I'm ready. I don't want to answer the phone anymore."

On our way up to the foundry Bud asked me if I was nervous. I laughed and said, "No, I don't have to be. Everyone else is nervous for me. I'm really excited!" We loaded Gabriel onto the truck and covered him with a sheet.

As we were standing next to the truck Bud looked at me with a sad look on his face. I asked him what was wrong? He said, "Nothing." Then he said with a sad voice, "Well, come on lets go so you can give my Angel away." His words pierced my heart.

"My' Angel" I thought to myself *"oh my, he doesn't want to give Gabriel away."* I found myself feeling very sad for him and realizing that he did believe me about

Gabriel after all. I could see the sadness on his face. I forced myself not to look at him. I knew if I did, I would cry.

The parade was beginning and all of my family and friends were there. Gabriel was on the truck covered with a big sheet. Everyone was very nervous except me. I kept laughing at them. They kept asking me, "What are you going to say?"

I would look at them and say, "I don't know yet?" This was making them even more nervous.

Finally the parade was over and Bud was ready to back the truck into the center of the street. The firemen were starting to congregate. Then all of a sudden the fire whistle blew. All of the firemen took off running to get to their trucks. I stood there thinking *Well Gabriel this is what it is all about.*

Everyone came up to me and said,
"What are you going to do now?"
 "Well, I guess we will just have to wait
until tonight to give it to them. After all that
was what I originally was going to do
anyway." I said. But for a lot of reasons, I
was asked to give him to the firemen after
the parade."
I went to the announcement booth and
announced that I would be giving this gift to
the firemen at 8.00 P.M. tonight.

 I asked Bud what we were going to do with
Gabriel until tonight? I suggested that we
could take him back to the foundry. Bud
said, "No, we would just leave him on the
truck covered with the sheet." Just then one
of the firemen (who didn't go on the run with
the others) came up to us and told us that we
could leave the truck over by the beer tent
and he would make sure no one messed
around with it. So that is what we did.

Then we went home to wait.

It was 6.00 P.M. when we decided it was time to head back uptown. When we arrived, Honey came up to me and asked what we were going to do? I told her that we were going to put Gabriel up on the stage where the band was going to be playing. I asked Jim (Honey's husband) if he would help Bud lift Gabriel up on the stage. The stage was a half-open semi-trailer, so they had to lift him pretty high. They did it with out a problem.

I then walked over to the DJ and asked the man if he would play the *Angels Among Us* Song for me after I had said a few words to the firemen. He agreed, then he programmed his equipment so he would be ready.

I walked over to one of the tables where my family and friends were sitting.

Everyone started bugging me about when I was going to give Gabriel away. I kept telling them 8.00 P.M. just like I said before. Then everyone wanted to know what I was going to say? I told them I had no idea and that I would think of something. I noticed Honey smiling at me. I asked her what she was smiling about?

She started laughing and said, "You're going to kill me!"

I felt a knot forming in my stomach. I knew she had done what I asked he not too. She was now looking beyond me and laughing harder. I was afraid to turn around for fear of what I would see. She rose from her chair and walked off. I stayed seated then looked at my sisters. They also were smiling from ear to ear. I felt like crying. I wanted to get up and go home.

I said to my Mom, "Please don't tell me that she called the TV station."

Mom smiled and said, "Joy, you didn't think that we would let this day go by without calling them did you?"

"Yes, I said, because I asked you guys not to!"

I turned around and saw Honey walking over to me with a cameraman. I felt sick. "Well I'm not going to talk to him!" I said.

My dad walked up to me and said, "Yes you are. I called them also and they said that they had gotten several calls about this. So we are not the only ones who think this is news worthy." I shook my head and looked at the ground.

Honey walked up to me with the reporter. He introduced himself to me and said, "I would like to do an interview with you."

"And what do you want me to say?" I asked him.

"I will ask you some questions and you answer them, ok?" he said.

I looked at him then at my family, they were all waiting expectantly for my reply.

"Well I guess it all depends on what questions you ask."

He said, "I understand you are nervous, but it will be ok."

"No, I am not nervous," I answered. "I just don't want to do this!"

He didn't know what to say. He stood there for a moment then said, "Well, I tell you what, if you don't like the way the interview goes then we will not air it, ok?" Everyone was still staring at me, waiting for me to answer. I felt as if I couldn't breathe. I felt like an ant that was being looked at under a microscope. I just wanted to find a hole and crawl in it.

"Don't they understand this is not about me, it is about the firemen."

I looked at my mom and dad and my family. I could see how proud they were of me. Then my dad winked at me and nodded his head, yes. I could also see Gabriel standing next to him. He was also smiling. I could hear Gabriel saying,

"I am with you."

I knew at that moment I had to do the interview, for them and for Gabriel. I finally agreed. I looked at the reporter and said, "Make it short and sweet, Please!

My sisters came up and started fixing my hair. I told them I thought that I looked fine. "This is me!" I said. "If I don't look good enough, that is too bad. This day is not about me. It is about Gabriel and the firemen."

My fears were that people would think that I was doing the interview for my own publicity and that was far from the truth.

The interview started with the question why I made the angel for the firemen? I said, "Because they are *Our Guardian Angels*. No matter who we are, if we get in an accident or need them they are always there to try and save us if they can.

Like I said, they are *Our Earthly Guardian Angels.*"

The interview ended as fast as it began. I asked for short and sweet and it was. I was relieved when it was over, I could finally breathe.

It was now 7.30 P.M. My oldest children Ely and Leah came up to me and asked when I was going to give Gabriel away? I told them in half an hour. They told me that they would be back at 8.00 and took off. Meanwhile every two minutes someone would ask me, "When are you going to do it Joy? What are you going to say?" I was so overwhelmed by everybody's excitement, I felt as if everything was out of control. I found myself not being able to breathe again. I was finally tired of listening to them and yelled,

"RIGHT NOW!!! WILL THIS MAKE ALL OF YOU HAPPY?"

They all yelled back at me, "YES!" Everyone stared running around with excitement and telling each other that I was going to do it now. I walked over to the DJ and told him that I was almost ready. Then I headed for the stage.

As I walked up to the stage, I said a prayer that the right words would come out of my mouth. I asked Gabriel to be with me, but I already knew he was. I found myself wondering how the firemen were going to react. Bud was walking with me, he said, "What if they don't like or don't want Gabriel?" His words "don't want" stunned me. I thought to myself, *I never thought of that.*

I looked at Bud and said, "Well, then we will just take him back home with us."

Autumn and my niece Amber came with us so they could help take the sheet off

Gabriel when the music started. My mind was so preoccupied, I didn't even think that my other children weren't there yet.

I stood on stage and announced, *"Could I please have all of the firemen over here by the bandstand?"* There was little response. I could see people staring at me wondering what I just said.

So I said, ***"Fire Department we need you."***

My heart hit the floor. There was little response again. Finally, I saw them coming. One by one, following each other. They stood in front of me.

I said to them. *"The reason I called you guys over here is because I have a gift to give you. I was asked to make this for you because you guys are very dear and special to the community, and us. Without you we would be lost. We know; if we get in an accident you will be there. I know you have had a bad year and hopefully when you see this and you have another bad run, it will help. And you will know what you guys are to us.*"

I then looked at the DJ and nodded my head. I then said, "*So it is all yours. I don't know what you are going to do with it but here it is.*"

At that moment the song <u>Angels Among Us</u> Started playing and Autumn, Amber and Bud pulled the sheet off of Gabriel. I watched the men's reactions. Their eyes welled up with tears. They stood there with a look of awe on their faces. Some of them had tears running down their cheeks. I knew that they were happy with Gabriel. I had nothing left to say. I choked back my tears and turned to walk off the stage.

Bud said, "Joy, look." The men were still standing there looking at Gabriel with tears rolling down some of their faces. I started to cry myself. The emotions that were filling the air were overwhelming.

Just then the firemen silently walked up to the stage and reached up to grab Gabriel. Bud and I picked Gabriel up and moved him to the edge of the stage. Then we handed him down to them.

They picked him up and walked off towards the fire department. The song was still playing as they were carrying Gabriel home. It was a very emotional sight. I thought to myself, *"if they only knew how many times Gabriel and their Angels carried them and now they are proudly carrying Gabriel."*

It brought joy to my heart once again. The firemen walked in a group surrounding Gabriel. Some of them were clearing a path for the men, who were carrying Gabriel. It was a beautiful sight. I walked off the stage and went down to where my son Tyler was. He asked me, "Where are they taking Gabriel?" I looked at him through my tears

and said, "Home, they are taking him home."
After the firemen took Gabriel to the fire
hall, each one of them came to me and gave
me a hug and thanked me.
Some of them told me how much they
appreciated the statue.
Some of the men just hugged me and smiled
with tears in their eyes. This moment
needed no words. I understood completely.
My fears of the firemen not liking Gabriel
were gone. I knew that the healing had
already begun.

When I crawled into bed that night I was
emotionally exhausted. But this was a good
exhaustion. I thanked God and Gabriel in
my prayers for all the blessings I had
received and also for the beautiful day that
he had given me. I added to my prayers that
I would be more than glad to do more, if it
was Gods will. After saying my prayers, I
laid there for a few moments before I fell

asleep. In the back of my mind I thought about the other firemen and rescue workers that didn't belong to our fire department. I had flashbacks of the pain they endured. I felt so sad for them. I knew that there must be some way to get Gabriel to them, but I didn't have a clue as to how this was going to be done.

I knew that I couldn't possibly make that many statues. I wondered how they were going to learn about their Angel Gabriel? I said to God, "I will leave this up to you but if you decide this job is done then that will also be alright with me."

Throughout the rest of the year all was quiet. I often would try to think of ways to get Gabriel to the others that needed him, but all I could do when people asked was tell them of my experience and give them a picture of Gabriel. Throughout the year, I handed out over 500 picture of the statue of Gabriel that was taken on community day.

(A white Angel with a beautiful blue sky behind him, just like Adam had said)
I was satisfied knowing that I did my best for God and Gabriel and that my job was completed.

ANOTHER VISIT

It was January 1998. A year had gone by. I awoke to find Gabriel standing at my bedside again. He was as beautiful as he was the first time. Again he reached his hand out to me and I put mine in his. I stood beside him.

"There are many more who need me. Get me to them. They are everywhere, they are all over the world."

I said, Gabriel, the world? How can I reach people all over the world? I know the world is not a big place for you but to me, it is more than my mind can even begin to fathom.

"How?" I asked. "Do I make more statues?"

"It is all taken care of. Get me to them. They are all over the world."

With those words he disappeared as fast as he came, leaving me with another challenge.

I awoke the next day and told my husband that my job for Gabriel was not done yet and that I had more to do. Bud said, "Joy let it go. You are obsessed with this. Now that things have calmed down you want to keep it going. You did what you felt you had to do, but you have to let it go."
My heart broke with his disbelieving words. I looked at him and said, "You just don't get it do you?" Bud shook his head and walked outside.
I sat at my desk with tears in my eyes, thinking that maybe he was right.
Maybe I just couldn't let Gabriel go.

Maybe it was my imagination and Gabriel really didn't come to me again. I closed my eyes for a moment and I could see Gabriel just as I did before. I looked at my hands and felt the energy in them again. I had not felt this since I had given Gabriel to the firemen.

I went out to the barn where Bud was. I asked him, *"If I was obsessed with this, than why has it been so long? Why didn't I come up with something more before now? Why don't you believe me?"*

Bud shook his head. I knew that he was not going to respond to my questions.

I turned to go back to the house when Bud said, "Joy let it go." I didn't say another word I just walked away.

I thought to myself, *if I would have listened to others the last time, Gabriel's statue wouldn't be here now and he wouldn't be helping those who needed him.* As I walked through the door I realized that the glass in the door needed to be washed. I continued into the kitchen where there were some old newspapers sitting in a bag that my parents had brought over for the puppies. I grabbed a hand full of them along with the window cleaning solution then headed back to the door.

I said out loud, "Gabriel, I really need another sign from you about this if you want me to continue. So please hurry and tell me or show me before someone puts me into a insane asylum this time."

I crumbled up the papers and started washing the windows with one Newspaper after the other. I grabbed the last paper when I heard a voice say,

"Look at the paper."

I stood there for a moment, dumbfounded. I looked around the room. No one was there. I heard the voice again,

"Look at the paper."

My stomach was in knots. I was afraid to open the paper for fear of what I would see. I had not read the newspapers so I had no idea what was in them.

   I straightened out the paper that was in my hand and the headlines read,

"It has been a year and still the healing goes on."

It was a story about the plane crash and how the rescue workers and firemen were still healing. I grabbed the other papers that I had used.   They were soaked with window detergent. I opened them up one after the other. Each one was about the different fire departments and rescue departments that were at the site.

   Every one of the firemen said that they were still having nightmares about the whole ordeal. There were also the names of the people who had perished on the plane. As I read the papers, I had flashbacks of the scene that Gabriel had shown me with the people that were on the plane. I wanted to call and tell all of the people who had worked at the crash site not to be sad. I wanted to call all the crash victims' families and share this whole experience with them, so they could be at peace.

But I knew that if I did this, everyone would think that I was some kind of nut. I looked for the name of the people that were on the plane. When I read their names for the first time, I had another flashback. I saw their faces again, and there expressions of when they saw the Angels coming for them. My emotions ran away with me and I started to cry. My tears were of happiness. For the people who died and because I knew that I had been given the sign that I asked for.

I unfolded all the news papers that I had used and laid them across the back of the couch to dry. Bud walked in and asked me what I was doing?

I could hardly talk. I felt as if I had been struck by lighting. I finally gathered my emotions and answered him. "Look at theses papers. I asked for a sign and once again I got it. The whole paper is about the rescue people and the plane crash."

Then I said, "Do you think this is my imagination? Or is it a sign?"

Bud just stared at me. I answered my own question to him before he could say a word, adding, "I say it is a sign. So you see, there is more that I have to do. And I'm not obsessed."

Bud said, "I didn't mean to hurt your feelings but you have to admit, this whole thing has been very strange."

"Yes it has," I agreed, "But if you think it has been strange for *you,* well than you should be *me*!"

I now knew that Gabriel had more for me to do, but I didn't know what.

People started asking me to make small statues of Gabriel. I thought that maybe this was what he wanted me to do. So I sculpted a small version of the big statue. 12 inches tall. They turned out beautiful. But I just knew that somehow this was not what Gabriel had in mind.

ANSWERED PRAYERS

It was now February of 1998.
I was looking on the Internet for web sites
about Angels. I wanted to see if I could find
someone who had an experience something
similar to my experience with Gabriel. I ran
across a web site that had Angel stories on
it. I eagerly read each one. I thought they
were wonderful stories, but none of them
were quite like my experience.

I then noticed that you could write your
story and get feedback from a lady, so I
thought I would be brave and write
something short and sweet. I briefly told her
my story without going into much detail, just
enough to explain part of what had
happened.

The next day she e-mailed me and asked if
there was something she could do for me. I
told her that I didn't know at this time but
that I was trying to write my story down.

She asked me why I felt that I needed to wright my story?

I told her, "People need to understand what Gabriel is all about. And if I tell my story I'm sure this would help people." Besides I added, they need to understand that this statue of Gabriel represents so much. He is more than just a statue of an Angel, and writing a book is the only way that I know how to get Gabriel's story out to people. If I tell everything that happened then people will understand."

She told me that she was a writer and that she would be glad to write it for me. I told her that I would have to think about it.

I was concerned about giving my story or anything to anyone, especially over the Internet.

Not too long after I had conversed with this lady, she said that there were two ladies that she thought could be of help. And asked if it would be ok for them to contact me. She said one of them was Linda Daly and she was from Redford, Michigan the Detroit area. Linda had read my letter that I had sent in. Then there was Paula Hunter, she is from England. She had sent photos to this lady that she had taken on a snowy day in England and the pictures look like there are Angels in them. We met on a chat line some days later.

They wanted to know all about my experience with Gabriel, then they asked if there was anything they could do for me. I told them that I didn't know. After our chat we started to email each other daily.

Linda, Paula and I wrote back and forth and got to know each other. One day Linda called me and asked if I would mind if she came to my house since we only lived 1 hour away from each other. She wanted to go to the Firehouse and see Gabriel. When she arrived it was as if we were old friends.

She wanted to hear the whole story.

I told her everything from beginning to end. Before she left Linda told me that her son was a volunteer fire fighter in another state and that he was supposed to be on the flight that had crashed, but he missed his flight. She told me of the horror she felt when she heard about the plane's misfortune. And about how relieved she was when her phone rang and it was her son. He had called to tell her that he had missed his flight. She added that she wanted to thank me for what I was doing for the firemen.

I told Linda that I thought the thanks should go to God and Gabriel not to me. "I am just doing as I was asked to do." I told her. Linda said she understood this but if I had not listened to my calling then Gabriel still wouldn't be here.

"Yes he would I said, he would have found someone else to do this for him."

I showed Linda the small clay figure of Gabriel I had made and another one that I was working on for a key chain. I asked her what she thought about key chains for the rescue workers?

Linda told me that she thought the men wouldn't carry something like that. I had to agree with her. When she was leaving, I told her that if she came up with any ideas about how we could get Gabriel to the other fire departments and other earthly angels, to let me know. She said she would.

AN IDEA

Linda called me on her way home from her car phone. She said, "Joy, I have an idea. What do you think about prayer cards with Gabriel on them? They would be small enough that the firemen and women could carry them in their wallets or pockets if they chose to. And they could always have Gabriel on them."

I said that sounded like a great idea but wondered how we could do this. I also asked, how much this would cost. Linda laughed and said, "Joy, I'm a printer by trade. I have everything that I need at home to make them. All we need is a prayer."

I laughed and said, "Linda, now I know why you were sent to me. God hand picked you."

Linda said with excitement, "I will start working on them right away when I get home. I will use the picture of Gabriel that you gave me for the front of them."

A couple of days later Linda called, she said she wanted to read me a prayer that her husband Bill wrote. Her voice was quivering. I could tell she was full of emotion.

The prayer read:
Dear Heavenly Father,
Through the guidance and wisdom of your Angelic Messenger Gabriel, grant me the strength to continue to face the challenges that lie before me. Keep me from Harms Way and protect me from my own insecurities and doubts, so I may continue to Serve You and My Fellow Man. Amen

A chill ran down my spine as she read this to me. "Oh my Linda! That is beautiful and perfect.

Where did you find the prayer?" I asked.

"My husband Bill walked into the room as I was working on the front of the cards. I asked him what he thought about them and he didn't answer me so I asked him again. He still didn't answer me. I turned around to see what he was doing and he asked me for a paper and pen. I asked him why and he said, "Just give me a pen and paper, before I lose my thought." When I did, he started to write.

When he was done he handed the paper to me and this is the prayer he wrote. "Joy!" "Isn't it just perfect? Isn't it just beautiful?"

"Yes it is." I agreed.

Linda said she had asked Bill where he came up with the prayer. He told her it just came into his head and he knew that he Had to write it down before he forgot it. I asked Linda to ask Bill if it would be ok to use his prayer on the back of the cards.

She said, "Of course!"

Then Linda said, Joy you just don't understand.
For Bill to come up with something like this he had to be inspired by something or someone. This was truly Heaven Sent."

This is how the prayer and prayer card's came about.

Linda worked on the cards day and night to get them just right, and when they were, the printing began. With in two months she printed over 1,500 of them and sent them to me. I bought a laminator and started laminating them. We gave all of them away.
We found that we were having a hard time keeping up with the demand and I hadn't started sending them to the fire departments yet. All of the cost came out of our pockets. We never asked for money for the cards. We would just give them away to people who wanted or needed them.

I never wanted anyone to say that I was doing this for the money. I knew that Gabriel would take care of us.

When money would get tight and I didn't think I could afford to keep the cards going. I would get $10.00 or $20.00 in the mail and a note saying, "This is to help with the printing cost." This would inspire me to keep going. I made up a letter to the firemen trying to explain the best I could to them about Gabriel without sounding like I was some crazy woman. I put a prayer card in each letter and sent them off to the fire departments in my surrounding area. I started out with the Ida fire department, then all of the ones that were involved with the plane crash.

In my heart I felt that it was very important to get Gabriel to them. I knew that someone needed him there. I sent the letters and cards to other fire departments as well. I wanted to get the cards to everyone who was

I never wanted anyone to say that I was doing this for the money. I knew that Gabriel would take care of us.

When money would get tight and I didn't think I could afford to keep the cards going. I would get $10.00 or $20.00 in the mail and a note saying, "This is to help with the printing cost." This would inspire me to keep going. I made up a letter to the firemen trying to explain the best I could to them about Gabriel without sounding like I was some crazy woman. I put a prayer card in each letter and sent them off to the fire departments in my surrounding area. I started out with the Ida fire department, then all of the ones that were involved with the plane crash.

In my heart I felt that it was very important to get Gabriel to them. I knew that someone needed him there. I sent the letters and cards to other fire departments as well.

I wanted to get the cards to everyone who was at the site and the family members who lost family members there, but I had no idea how to go about this for the family members. Unfortunately, I still have no idea how to reach them. My goal is to get Gabriel's prayer cards to all the Earthly Guardian Angels out there and also to anyone who would like them.

Gabriel has done what he said he would. He has reached people through the prayer cards all over the world.

Paula started getting the cards off to the rest of the world. She has distributed hundreds of them in England. And people from England have sent them on to other parts of the world.

As of today the cards have been sent to England, Australia, Portugal, Equador, Filipinos, Belgium, Germany and all over the U.S.A.

My Reflections:

As I was writing this book, I thought about the whole experience once again. I feel very blessed to be an instrument for God. But I do not feel special in anyway because we are all instruments if we just follow the path that is laid out for us.

I know that I am leaving out little things that have slipped through my thoughts, as it has been two years since this whole thing started. But I can assure you that Gabriel's work still continues on even today.

The Summerfield Fire Department in Petersburg Michigan has put Gabriel up on their roof and encased him in glass. At night he has lights on him. I must say when I go by the firehouse and see him, at night or day, it still takes my breath away.

God Bless you and may His Heavenly Angels be there to guide you across life's good bridges and the broken ones.

I want to thank Lynn, Sandy, Adam, John and Thad, once again. Without your guidance, wisdom, and help, none of this could have been possible. I love you all. And may God always give you special blessings. Thank you for being some of Gods Earthly Angels.

One last thing, We must remember to thank the people who look out for us. A simple word like Thank you, to someone who puts their life on the line to save yours, gives them what they need to go on to save someone else. So the next time you see an Earthly Guardian Angel give them a smile and let them know you care.

And to All of you Earthly Guardian Angel's that put your lives on the line everyday for us. Please know that I say a special prayer for you everyday. What more can I say to you but
                    Thank you.

To order prayer cards for your Fire, Rescue, Police or other Departments.

Send the <u>Name of the department…</u> <u>Address…City…Statue…Zip code…</u> (Country) if outside the U.S.A.
And approximately how many cards will be needed…

To: Joy LaPlante
       P.O. Box 112
       Petersburg, Michigan 49270

Or: Email me at: angels@cass.net

       There is no charge for this.

You can also add your own letter to go with the cards. Just send it along with the information above. I will send it with the cards. Thank you.

How to get prayer cards for yourself

If you would like a prayer card for yourself, or someone who has touched your life. All you have to do is send me:

A self-addressed <u>Stamped</u> envelope With your name and address on it to the address on the previous page.

Please Note: I can only send 3 cards to an envelope.

Good News: You may send me as many envelope's as you wish.

There is no charge for the cards, but donations are excepted. Each card cost around 45 cents to make so any donation is greatly appreciated.

Thank you, and may God Bless you.

For information on small statues of Gabriel

Send a self addressed <u>Stamped</u> envelope to my address on the opposite page. I will send you a brochure.

Thank you.